Communication for Couples

An Essential Guide: Hear Your Partner to Achieve a Healthy Relationship, Improve Mindful Habits and Grow Empathy for Each Other

I0222503

© Copyright 2019 - All rights reserved.

This eBook is provided with the sole purpose of providing relevant information on a specific topic for which every reasonable effort has been made to ensure that it is both accurate and reasonable. Nevertheless, by purchasing this eBook, you consent to the fact that the author, as well as the publisher, are in no way experts on the topics contained herein, regardless of any claims as such that may be made within. As such, any suggestions or recommendations that are made within are done so purely for entertainment value. It is recommended that you always consult a professional before undertaking any of the advice or techniques discussed within.

This is a legally binding declaration that is considered both valid and fair by both the Committee of Publishers Association and the American Bar Association and should be considered as legally binding within the United States.

The reproduction, transmission, and duplication of any of the content found herein, including any specific or extended information will be done as an illegal act regardless of the end form the information ultimately takes. This includes copied versions of the work both physical, digital and audio unless express consent of the Publisher is provided beforehand. Any additional rights reserved.

Furthermore, the information that can be found within the pages described forthwith shall be considered both accurate and truthful when it comes to the recounting of facts. As such, any use, correct or incorrect, of the provided information will render the Publisher free of responsibility as to the actions taken outside of their direct purview. Regardless, there are zero scenarios where the original author or the Publisher can be deemed liable in any fashion for any damages or hardships that may result from any of the information discussed herein.

Additionally, the information in the following pages is intended only for informational purposes and should thus be thought of as universal. As befitting its nature, it is presented without assurance regarding its continued validity or interim quality. Trademarks that are mentioned are done without written consent and can in no way be considered an endorsement from the trademark holder.

Table of Contents

Introduction

Congratulations on downloading the book *Communication for Couples,* and thank you for doing so. The information you find in this book can be put to practice as soon as one wants to. Communication is a task that many people take lightly and assume is easy and does not require much effort. However, one must realize that good communication requires attention and effort, especially for couples.

Downloading this book is the first effort you have made to understanding perfect communication for couples. This first step is the easy part. The information you will find in the following chapters is so crucial that you should take it to heart and apply it in your day to day life. If you do not need the information as at yet, file the tips away and use them when needed. You will be glad that you gathered the information and that you can use the tips.

To that end, the chapters in this book will discuss how empathy is the basis for good communication, empathic listening, the importance of working on yourself first, diplomatic dialogue skills, developing mindful habits, appreciating and accepting your partner for what he or she, the ego monster, loving unconditionally, setting common goals, growing together, and the importance of practicing day after day to achieve a mindful relationship.

There are many books in the market that address the matter of communication for couples, so thank you again for choosing this one. Every effort has been made to make sure that the book delivers valuable and useful information to you. Please enjoy!

Chapter 1: What is empathy?

Empathy refers to the ability to sense the emotions of other people combined with the ability to understand and imagine what they might be feeling or thinking. Not everybody can understand and empathize with other people. Empathy is the basis for good communication.

Some days back, while we were going home from a meeting, we found a homeless woman standing at the corner of the street shaking because of the cold. Her clothes were too thin to protect her from the chilly weather, and she looked weary. In front of her was a signboard that said, "Please help. I will truly appreciate it." As we walked by, most of us stopped to give the woman some dollars. However, one woman, a wife to an acquaintance stood back in disgust and ranted that the homeless people were just lazy. She went ahead to mention that the homeless people were freeloaders who had acquired the skill of offloading people by playing with their emotions. She also dared to say that probably, the homeless woman collected more money from people than her salary. Our male colleague was so embarrassed by the character of his wife until he averted his eyes.

Why is it that some people can feel and understand the suffering of others while others cannot? How is it that some people can remain so cold to others to the extent of being indifferent and uncaring while others can envision the problems, empathize, and even look for ways to help them?

Generally, human beings are well attuned to their own emotions and feelings. As such, people are wired to identify what they and their colleagues are going through. However, it requires empathy for us to be able to walk in the shoes of other people and helping them so to speak. Empathy supports the human ability to understand the emotions and feeling the other person is experiencing. For many people, it is easy to respond with kindness and gentleness to people who are undergoing challenges and as such, showing hostility to an already troubled person is incomprehensible. However, like in the case mentioned earlier scenario, it is not everyone who can empathize with other people; we can, therefore, say that empathy is not a thing that applies to all people all the time.

So, what does empathy entail? In the year 1909, psychologist Edward B. Titchener introduces the term empathy from the German word 'einfühlung.' The word 'einfühlung' can be defined as 'feeling into.' It refers to the ability to emotionally and psychologically understand the experiences of another person. Mostly, one gets to the position of the other person and somehow feels what they must be going through. The word empathy is used to refer to a variety of experiences depending on the context. For instance, Emotional researchers define the term as the ability to imagine the thoughts and feelings of another combined with the ability to sense the emotions involved.

On the other hand, contemporary researchers look at empathy from 2 angles; Affective empathy and cognitive empathy. Affective empathy refers to the feelings and sensations that one gets in response to the emotions of the other person. It may involve feeling stressed and anxious because someone else is suffering. Cognitive empathy is the ability to understand and identify the feelings of other people. Scientists have found that some experiences, conditions, and disorders make it hard for some people to empathize.

Empathy has been found to have some deep roots in the brains and bodies of human beings and other animals. Many studies in neuroscience suggest that empathy is found in both human beings and animals. It can be linked to a majority of mammals. For instance, dolphins have been seen to save humans and other creatures from drowning or being eaten by sharks. Animals as big as an elephant have shown most of the characteristics of empathy and compassion towards each other and also to other creatures. Behavior studies of the primates in the wild as well as in captivity have indicated that they are empathic and more so the Bonobos.

Closer to home, the dogs have shown elements of empathy and so have rats. Remember that having empathy does not necessarily mean that one wants to help the people in trouble although this is usually the first vital step towards compassionate actions. The empathy experience normally facilitates the pro-social behavior of the ability to help others without being forced. Empathy promotes a level of compassion that is different for every individual. Most people desire to be listened to with compassion and understanding, and they want the listener to feel beyond the words. Empathy demonstrates care to such people.

In most cases, empathy is an excellent thing when applied well. It increases positivity, principles and high ethical standards. However, some people say that too much empathy interferes with the rational thinking capacity of an individual. Too much empathy may have detrimental effects on the individual and the world at large. When people lead too much with the heart rather than the head, they tend to lose the big picture, and they feel the long term consequences of over empathy.

We should note that empathizing with another person does not mean that the emotional state of the empath matches the other person in every detail. Rather, empathy implies that we share and understand the feelings, experiences, and emotions of the other person using our mind to simulate the scenes based on our past experiences. For example, if someone is ill, we understand their pain by associating their experience to our past events of sickness.

Given that human beings use their feelings and experiences as the model for sharing and understanding the experiences of other people, some researchers say that empaths engage both emotional and the cognitive process in feeling and thinking about the experience of the other person. Scientific studies show that in many cases, the medial prefrontal cortex shows robust activation as soon as we think (cognitively) about the feelings and emotions of other people. However, the studies also show that the central regions of the same prefrontal cortex show superior activation of the emotion-angle taking tasks compared to the cognitive perspective. This analysis of the brain suggests that the ventral part may be involved more in affective (feeling) processing while the dorsal region handles the more challenging task of cognitive (thinking) processing.

We can, therefore, say that once a person starts empathizing with someone, he/she uses the cognitive processes to try and analyze the emotional state. Next, the person imagines himself/herself in a particular state by drawing on the emotional memories he/she had in the past. Ultimately, the person embodies the emotions he/she is imagining. As we try to understand how the seemingly complex process of empathy develops and why it is that people and even other animals are emotionally affected by the experiences of others, scientists have identified two potential precursors namely, imitation and emotional contagion. Imitation refers to the establishment of correspondence between the behavior one person and another. For instance, newborn babies will tend to copy their parents in an effortful and consistent way beginning with simple acts like sticking out a tongue. Imitation does not force one to change the emotional state, but it gives one the opportunity to learn how and when certain feelings occur. From imitation, people become better at processing the feelings of others.

On the other hand, emotional contagion is defined as the tendency to directly or indirectly catch the emotions of the other person. For instance, a baby might start crying just because he/she has had another one cry. These contagions can occur unconsciously and outside our awareness. We cannot say that imitation and emotional contagion are the only precursors of empathy, but it is evident that behavioral and biological mechanisms underlying the two aspects overlap with the process of empathy. We can also say that empathy, imitation, and emotional contagion contributes to pro-social behavior. All three constructs are found in human beings and many animals, but empathy is more evident in people than animals because it requires higher degrees of emotional and cognitive processing.

Summarily, empathy is the bedrock of close connection and intimacy. If we did not have empathy, relationships would be so emotionally shallow that shared activities and mutual interests would be the only common aspects between people. Again, if human beings did not have empathy, they would work together but never really understand the feelings of each other and even the inner selves. Life would be like being in a subway with total strangers who have no idea what the other person is about. Empathy does not only fuel pro-social behavior and closeness, but also, it helps people to stop when they act up because of the awareness of the pain and bad emotions they might be causing. Empathy puts breaks on excessive self-interest; otherwise, we would have scorched earth. Please note that empathy and sympathy do not have a similar meaning.

Chapter 2: Empathic Listening (Using Empathy to listen to your partner)

Psychologists have found that human beings are wired for empathy by the deep attachment relationships developed in the two early years of life. Studies have revealed that 18-month-olds are able to put themselves in the shoes of someone else to some extent. This empathy does not stop developing once people have grown up; rather, people nurture its growth throughout life. As such, empathy becomes a radical force supporting social transformation.

Different people have different levels of empathy and scholars have classified them accordingly. For example, there are people who have a complete lack of empathy. Such people find it very hard to maintain relationships and have no contact with remorse. They cannot understand how another person is feeling, and they may or may not be cruel. Some of the people identified under this category include narcissistic individuals, psychopaths, and borderline personalities.

Other categories of empaths include (1) those who have empathy but lack self-control such that they easily hurt people when they are upset, (2) those who have difficulties with empathy but they have enough empathy to understand the impact of their actions after they have hurt someone, and (3) those who have a difficult time showing and having empathy because they know they do not see things as other people do and are never quite normal. Normal men tend to have low amounts of empathy, and in most cases, they avoid talking about emotions and as such, they base friendships on shared activities. Women, on the other hand, tend to have an above average level of empathy and they apply care when dealing with other people and stay sensitive to their feelings.

Have you ever realized how some people make you feel understood and validated without saying anything? What is the secret about them that makes it so simple for you to 'open up' and share your problems? Why are they the first person you go to whenever you want to unburden your soul? The answer to this question is simple – empathic listening.

That is what makes them the ideal conversation partners. It's the reason why everyone else seems to gravitate around them. It's why they get along well with everyone in the office and can click almost instantly with every person they meet.

In case you didn't know, empathic listening is an ability which means it can be learned through practice and repetition. And that's precisely what you're going to get out of this article.

Empathy: the cornerstone of authentic human interactions

In a world where time is a scarce resource and everyone seems to be running after something, it has become increasingly difficult for many of us to exercise patience and listen to others, before we express our own opinions and desires.

We expect others to understand us without ever putting ourselves in their shoes. We want others to resonate with our views without giving them a chance to voice their opinions. And even if they do express their views or offer some constructive criticism, we rarely return the favor.

As a result, our day-to-day interactions can become nothing more than a 'cold' exchange of replies; no 'real' connection, no empathy. But it doesn't have to be that way. If you are willing to listen instead of talk, understand instead of criticizing, and comfort instead of judging, you can quickly turn a conversation into an authentic human interaction.

Whether you're talking to your spouse, friend, boss, coworker, neighbor or even the barista who works at your favorite coffee shop, empathic listening can significantly improve the quality of your interaction. Contrary to popular belief, it was collaboration, not competition that helped humankind survive, thrive, and reach the level of socio-economic development we see today. And one of the keys to an authentic and fruitful collaboration is empathic listening.

What is empathic listening?

In a nutshell, empathic listening means to hear your conversation partner authentically. It's the ability to listen with the sincere intention of understanding other people's values, opinions, and ideas.

Empathic listening allows you to get 'in tune with their frequency' and resonate on an emotional level. It means to get in touch with their needs and make them feel heard.

Empathic listening opens a window to their inner universe and creates a safe space where they can share anything without having to worry about criticism or bad remarks.

When empathy is the bridge that brings two people together, words become less important and what matters most is the connection between them.

But being empathetic does not mean you have to agree with everything and does not imply any obligation on your part. It only involves an effort to understand other people's perspective; 'to walk a mile in their shoes' so to speak.

Sadly, not all people are naturally born with empathy; not everyone finds it easy to identify, process, and resonate with other people's emotions. However, we can develop and sharpen this skill through patience and exercise. Those of us who are disconnected from our feelings will find it a bit difficult, but not impossible to learn to improve empathy. Just as any other ability, empathic listening can be acquired, as long as you're motivated and willing to take it stepwise and practice consistently.

How does empathic listening relate to happiness?

Some of you may be wondering how exactly does listening to others and trying to resonate emotionally with them contribute to our well-being. What does empathic listening have to do with happiness?

First of all, empathetic ears are hard to come by these days. Many people are too self-involved to care about what others have to say. But given that healthy social interactions are critical to our growth, knowing how empathize is one of the ingredients of a happy and fulfilling life.

Second, research suggests that when you listen in an empathic manner, people are satisfied with the conversation and you instantly become more socially attractive. And since we're all social creatures by nature, being able to navigate social situations successfully will indirectly contribute to our overall sense of happiness and well-being.

Finally, given that empathic listeners are social magnets, they often benefit from exciting opportunities that contribute to their personal and professional growth. Overall, empathic listening can significantly add to our overall sense of happiness and well-being. Perhaps this is the secret to lasting joy and whole fulfilling life.

Empathic listening for couples

Empathic communication is an essential component of any successful and lasting relationship. The ability to be empathetic towards your loved one has significant effects on the overall level of satisfaction you and your partner experience in your relationship.

As you can imagine, knowing how to listen with an open mind - without interruptions, criticism, and unwanted advice – is a 'must' in any healthy and functional couple.

Too often, people who love each other end up splitting because of communication issues. Whether it manifests as stonewalling, criticism, or contempt, lack of empathy can slowly turn two people into two strangers who resent each other.

And that's because one of our fundamental needs is to be heard and understood. When this does not happen, you begin to feel lonely and abandoned. You suffer and eventually distance yourself, even from a person you loved more than you could ever imagine.

Experts suggest empathic listening paves the way for affectionate communication, a crucial element for any healthy couple. When empathic listening becomes a habit that characterizes your relationship, you can easily resonate with your partner's struggles and understand why he/she might be feeling that way. And this gives you the chance to find solutions and fix the 'cracks' that could compromise your relationship.

All and all, empathic listening builds strong relationships, fosters effective communications, and cultivates trust between life partners.

Empathic listening at work

In a way, we could argue that empathic listening is a 21st-century skill.

That means we not only use it to achieve personal growth by cultivating a thriving social life and building lasting romantic relationships, but also to advance in our career by investing in fruitful partnerships.

From leadership and business to sales and negotiation, empathy seems to be one of those variables that can tip the scale in your favor, overcome 'formal' barriers, and appeal to people's 'soft' side.

Empathic listening plays such an important role in activities like sales that researchers have even begun developing tools to measure it. One example is the active empathic listening (AEL) scale which evaluates three dimensions: sensing, processing, and responding. More specifically, this scale assesses how well the person can zero-in on emotions, process them, and come up with an appropriate answer.

If you wish to become a better boss, leader, coworker

or even employee, empathic listening should be among your 'sharpest' skills. Just because you talk to your boss, client, business partner, or coworker doesn't mean you should keep the conversation at a formal level. Appeal to their emotions, make them feel understood, and you will be on the right path towards a productive partnership.

In time, empathic listening can set the stage for fantastic business opportunities which directly contribute to a happy and prosperous life.

How to practice empathic listening?

Since developing empathic listening is all about practice, let's focus on a brief example that will show you how proper empathic communication should look like.

Mary: So, what's new in your life?

James: Hmm, nothing much.

Mary: You seem a bit off. Is everything ok? **(She detects a negative emotional vibe and uses a question to dig deeper)**

James: Just some minor problems with Mary; nothing so important.

Mary: You want to talk about it? I'm here for you. Maybe I can help you out in some way. **(She makes herself available and lets him know he can rely on her)**

James: I don't remember, things haven't been right between us lately.

Mary: I'm sorry to hear that. I don't want to be too

nosy, but did something happen between you two? **(She asks open-ended questions but without being intrusive)**

James: Well, I don't know if I should burden you with my problems.

Mary: It's ok. Don't worry. If you feel like sharing, I'm here for you **(She creates a safe space)**

James: Hmmm, things kind of went south about a month ago when I noticed she was texting with a guy from work. Although she told me there's nothing between them and I should stop making a big deal out of it, I can't help but think she might be having an affair with this guy.

Mary: So, because she's texting with this guy from work, you're worried it might be more between them? **(She paraphrases to make sure she got the message right and make him feel understood)**

James: Yes. And I know it sounds crazy, but I can't get this idea out of my head. God, I'm such a mess! I love her so much, but I'm afraid I'm going to lose her because of my stupid jealousy.

Mary: Look, James, I know you love Mary, and I know you don't want to lose her. Maybe that's why you're acting so jealous. **(She paraphrases his message, empathizes with him)**

Mary: But are there any other reasons you think she might be cheating on you? **(She asks open-ended questions to understand the situation further)**

James: Well, no. I don't think so. Maybe this whole cheating thing is just in my head.

Mary: Want some advice? **(She asks before giving advice)**

James: Sure.

Mary: Talk to your girl. Tell her what you told me. Tell her that you're acting this way because you love her and don't want to lose her. **(She encourages him to have a conversation with his girlfriend and clarify the situation)**

James: What if she doesn't understand? What if she thinks I'm crazy?

Mary: Then maybe you two could see a couple's counselor. Who knows? It might be the solution you need to fix this issue. **(She offers an alternative solution)**

James: I guess that could be an option. Thanks, Mary; it was constructive talking to you.

Mary: My pleasure! And thanks for placing your trust in me. If you ever need an empathetic ear, I'm here for you. **(She validates his confidence and extends her support)**

9 strategies to develop empathic listening

1. it's not about you

Whenever you're talking to someone and wish to lend an empathetic ear, the first thing you need to understand is that it's not about you.

That's the secret to authentic empathic listening – placing your conversation partner above your needs.

And it can be quite hard to put aside personal opinions

and make it all about him/her. After all, you're not his/her therapist.

So, before you decide to be there for someone, make sure you're available emotionally. Otherwise, there's no point in encouraging him or her to share a personal issue for which you're not ready to provide understanding and support.

2. Put away your phone

Too often we find ourselves checking our phone or answering a text message while the other person may be pouring their heart out.

This is one of those unpleasant habits that many of us have adopted as a result of living in the digital era. We get so hooked on social media that we sometimes end up losing sight of the person who's right there in front of us.

And it's impossible to establish an emotional bond when you're regularly checking your phone, and all you can say is *"Aha"* or *"I understand."* So, whenever you wish to offer empathy and create an authentic connection put your phone away and asks the other person to do the same.

3. Be an active listener

In a way empathic listening and active listening are synonymous. Being an active listener means being present in the conversation. It means ignoring any distractions and focusing exclusively on the person in front of you.

Active listeners live in the 'here and now.' They immerse themselves into the other person's universe and seek to gain a better understanding of the topic in discussion.

Of course, that doesn't mean you have to listen and nod in silence. A conversation is a two-way street where both partners exchange ideas, impressions, and seek to resonate with one another emotionally.

In short, active listening is about presence and depth.

4. Refrain from criticism

As you can probably imagine, empathic listening implies a high degree of emotional intelligence. When someone shares a story or event that holds significance to him/her, it would be ideal to refrain from evaluations, criticism, or negative feedback.

There are times when other people's problems may seem trivial, ridiculous, or even infuriating. But once again, it's not about you, it about them. Remember, your goal is to understand and provide emotional support. Any form of criticism will only create tension and make it difficult for you to 'forge' authentic connections. Listen, understand, and empathize.

5. Adjust your body language

As you probably know, body language is of paramount importance for genuine social interactions. When it comes to empathic listening, your body can help you create the kind of communication that makes room for understanding and empathy.

Your posture and gestures can either bring people closer or create a barrier that makes it difficult for you to listen actively and empathically.

If you want to make people feel safe and welcome, make sure to adopt a relaxed posture with open arms and constant eye contact. You can even go for a friendly pat on the shoulder or even a warm hug.

6. Paraphrase your conversation partner

Paraphrasing is among the most effective strategies for empathic listening. Letting your conversation partner know that you understand his perspective creates an ideal climate for sharing emotions.

Many studies suggest that paraphrasing – along with clarifying, questioning, and remembering details – are the critical elements of empathic listening. Furthermore, this creates a safe space where people can share and engage in self-exploration. Paraphrasing your conversation partner is relatively easy. All you need to do is listening to what your partner has to say and rephrase his/her message.

7. Ask open-ended questions

If you want your conversation partner to share, you need to 'fuel' the conversation by asking open questions. Sometimes, people don't 'open up' that easily. Not everyone will be willing to talk to you openly, especially when it comes to personal problems. And that's why you need to give him or her a push by using questions that create opportunities for sharing.

Although smart questions can enrich a conversation, make sure you're not intrusive. You're supposed to have a happy talk, not an interview.

If you notice that your partner doesn't feel comfortable, refrain from asking questions and let him or her dictate the flow of the conversation.

8. Stop giving unsolicited advice

When you're looking to establish an emotional connection with someone, the worst thing you can do is offer unsolicited advice. Nothing 'kills' the vibe of a good conversation more than telling the other person what he or she should do. Remember that empathic listening is mostly about understanding and 'connectedness.' Sometimes, all it takes to establish an emotional connection is active listening.

If, however, you think you have a good piece of advice to offer, ask your conversation partner if he/she is interested in hearing it.

9. Don't 'fill up' the silence

Many of us tend to feel awkward during the occasional moments of silence that are specific to any conversation. But silence can be a powerful tool in establishing an authentic connection is you know how to use it. You can use silence to allow the other person to take charge of the conversation or give him/her enough time to process your input and come up with an answer.

And let's not forget that a conversation doesn't rely solely on a constant exchange of words. There's also your body language which through which you can express empathy and build an authentic connection.

The importance of empathic listening

Empathic listening is also called reflective listening or active listening. It is a way of listening and responding to others that enhances trust and mutual understanding. It is a vital skill for disputants and third parties as well because it makes it possible for the listener to accurately interpret the received message from the speaker and provide a relevant response. The response is a fundamental part of the process of listening and can be essential to the success of mediation or negotiation. Empathic listening has numerous benefits that include:

- It will build respect and trust

- Enables the conflicting parties to release their emotions

- It will reduce your tension

- It will create a safe and conducive environment for collaborative solving of problems

- It will encourage the surfacing of essential details

Strategies to develop empathetic listening

- It is not about you

- Put away your phone

- Be an active listener

- Refrain from criticism

- Adjust your body language

- Ask open-ended questions

- Paraphrase your conversation when talking to your partner

In summary:

All in all, empathic listening represents the foundation of effective communication and one of the secrets to lasting relationships.

When you're willing to put aside your personal views and seek to empathize with others, people will gravitate around you. That, in turn, will result in authentic relationships and fruitful business partnerships. Even if you are not a natural born empathy, you can still develop this skill as long as you're willing to:

- Make the conversation about the person in front of you

- Avoid distractions

- Listen actively and refrain from criticism or advice-giving

- Paraphrase and ask open-ended questions

- Adjust your body language

- Use silence to your advantage.

Listen empathically, and others will be drawn naturally to your social circle.

Chapter 3: The importance of work on yourself first

The couple is made of two people; both must be responsible for their balance first. Change yourself to the better if you want to help your partner to be a better person.

Everybody gets angry for one reason or the other. Whether it shows or not, we are all bound to feeling tension when people overstep their boundaries, or certain matters go wrong. In marriages, spouses can avoid showing anger to avoid conflict. They shove it down and let it go unnoticed.

However, hidden anger is just as bad as that which explodes because, at one point or the other, it will hurt the relationship. In most cases, the more one lets the arguments to go on, the more the distance between him/her and the partner grows. The longer it lasts, the harder it is for the couple to repair the relationship and at such points, people look for divorce papers.

As human beings, anger pushes us to say or do things that WE would not do in normal circumstances. We should remember that once words are said and actions are done, it is impossible to unsay or undo them. When we explode, we should be careful about how we deal with anger. The emotion of anger is not right or wrong by itself. The morality of emotions and feelings comes in question only when we react to what we are feeling. For example, feeling angry is okay but destroying things out of anger brings the morality aspect.

Causes of conflicts between couples

More often than not, human beings forget that they are

different and that each has a different opinion and view of things. This happens a lot in marriage because the love and attraction make the couple feel like they are one. Although marriage brings 'two people together to become one' their minds still differ, their backgrounds are different, their upbringing is different; therefore they cannot have the same opinions all the time.

Everyone has a different memory and perception, and there is no one right and standard way of thinking. Even when you know that your opinion is right, your line of thought and perspective is not the only right one. A couple consists of two people, and if it is only one person who keeps giving their opinion without considering the opinion of the other one, then the marriage is made up on one person. This means that there is no room in the marriage for the two people and thus the communication stops, and the marriage no longer functions properly.

There are many different ways of dealing with issues positively without having fights that will end up destroying the communication. Spouses do not have to strive to fix each other rather; they should look for ways to agree and disagree positively. A couple should constantly deal with unresolved anger and issues. Do not bottle up things, feelings, emotions, opinions et cetera even if it is for the sake of the other person. Letting thing go without sorting them out fast and soon only leads to deeper conflicts and more distance to the extent of everyone using a confrontational tone and attitude even when they should not.

How to deal with anger

Firstly, when a spouse is wrong, he/she should not hesitate to apologize. Words such as 'I am sorry' go a long way in making a partner reconsider their next words. When honesty is applied by the person apologizing, there is no more room for more arguments. Conceding defeat does not make one weak and apologizing helps to loosen tension which might have escalated to disconnection and complete lack of communication. Staying stubborn and trying to 'fix' a partner will not help solve anything. Standing a ground is only necessary when the couple will win together but if the victory belongs to one person, chances are a brick wall will grow between them. It is therefore important that everybody communicates effectively, practice saying the right things to each other, build one another, talk to each other and avoid talking at one another.

Communication as a cornerstone to work on yourself

If one were to go to a crowd of people and ask them to name the most important aspect of marriage, they would mention a variety of things including trust, honesty love et cetera. Every person has their understanding of love and marriage, and they have their preferences. Of course, all the aspects that the people would mention play a crucial role in marriages but communication is the centerpiece of all communication.

The way the two spouses communicate with each other, discuss their issues, encourage and build one another through communication is essential for the sustainment of a fulfilling marriage. One can say that communication is the vehicle that carries all the other aspects of marriage. Without communication, that is verbal and verbal; a spouse could not know whether to trust and be honest with their partners. Assumptions usually break the marriage. If one person loves the other and does not talk about it or at least show it in words, they will not succeed in marriage. To the spouses; if you love your partner, let them know through words and actions.

If the communication between two people is honest, then the chances of the relationship surviving are high. Communication is the cornerstone of all relationship; however, many people are not good at communicating. Other people do not know how to address matters in the right way. Spouses need to use certain communication channels to create a strong and caring atmosphere in their marriage. Love, honesty trust and other important parts of marriage are not meaningful by themselves. One must be able to express these aspects to give them meaning. The expression of love and care in marriage is what makes it worth envy. Showing love acting honestly and showcasing trust is where the magic of marriage lies. The ability to communicate with a spouse about how much they mean to each other is where a marriage graduates from good to great. One should remember that communication is more than speaking about things; it is also showing. Under the umbrella of communication between couples, we can identify verbal, non-verbal and physical acts.

Verbal communication between couples

Verbal communication is the easiest and most commonly used form of communication. Words are easy to use to a large extent. People like to hear things especially when they are nice. For instance, every spouse loves to be complemented through words 'you look very nice today,' 'I love you.' You are a great person with an amazing personality.' Effective communication requires one to be able to express their feelings to their spouse through words. If a couple loves each other so much yet they are unable to communicate the same through words; they might never know how much they mean to each other. Even when the actions show clearly that the spouses love one another, they still need to say it in words. Words will add value to the actions and vice versa. They will make the involved parties feel appreciated, loved, and sure about how the other person feels.

Along with all the compliments and expression of the positive, the spouses can express what they are not happy about through words. If a spouse is doing something that is offending the other, yet the offended person is silent about it, the offender will most probably continue with their habits. Silence does not help in most cases. If anything, lack of communication will keep hurting the couple. One cannot possibly go through life while holding all the dissatisfaction inside. Verbal communication will help one let it all out. However, when letting matters out, one should be tactful and careful. Care and warmth in communication are essential, especially when talking about matters that might bring disagreements. Couples should not wait too long before they say something about things bothering them. They should also not wait too long before telling each other that they care.

Nonverbal communication between couples

At some point in life, we have said something unpleasant or unfriendly to someone else. They might not have retaliated verbally, but they show their displeasure through facial expressions and actions either voluntarily or involuntarily. The offended person did not have to say a word to tell the story, but it all showed on their faces. Human beings share more with their faces and body than they would give credit.

Spouses should be aware of their facial expression and body language while talking to their partners to avoid giving off the wrong message. Human beings are capable of reading the body language of their partners even subconsciously. If for example, a couple is having a serious conversation and one person id hunched over and probably closed off, the other will detect a lack of vulnerability. Use the right facial and body language for every conversation. For example, if a couple s having a serious conversation, it is important that the two parties Face each other and keep their body language open without crossing the legs or arms. The body language should show that the person is listening keenly, taking note of the important things and is willing to work through the subject matter. Nonverbal cues are many, and they communicate to the partner either positively or negatively even without an exchange of words. Everyone should be conscious and thoughtful of how their body language brings out their thoughts.

Physical acts

Physical acts include making dinner, doing the laundry, taking out the garbage, and even getting ice-cream from the fridge for a pregnant wife. Physical actions are not things one can express through words. They are things that one does for their spouses to show them how much they care. IN DOING SUCH simple things, one is communicating with their partners about how much they mean to them without using words. This form of communication falls under the phrase "Actions speak louder than words." You could sing your spouse that you love them till your face turns blue, but it would not mean as much as making him/her dinner or replacing their old attire. The power of actions outdoes the power of saying I love you 300 times a day.

Having in mind that communication is important for the success of marriage; one cannot rely on just one of the ways mentioned above. Every spouse should strike a balance between the three to ensure that the marriage thrives. It is okay for a spouse to tell their partner that they love them and at the same time give an opinion about things that are bothering them. Open communication will benefit the marriage in the long term and become an investment to reap from. Every person should use body language to show their spouses that they are honest and open with them. An observant eye will pick negative body language no matter how well one hides it. A spouse may take this as a red flag for the beginning of the end of the marriage. Couples need to stay alert about what they communicate through their bodies and make appropriate adjustments so that the spouse can read honesty and trust

Again, a couple should use actions to communicate to their spouses A gift or two, a body massage, a dinner date, or even assisting with a troubling task can go a long way to communicate to each other. Actions will always speak for themselves; even if one was to keep singing that they love someone yet they fail to show it in actions, then they will fail. Without open and effective communication, a couple will face more challenges and obstacles than otherwise.

Chapter 4: Diplomatic dialogue skills

Diplomatic dialogue skills are a better way to talk while respecting your partner sensibility.

Is there one thing that can be defined as the key to a good marriage? It is hard to answer this question in one word. Every marriage is different; the couples have different things that keep them and their relationship successful. Whether the couple is newly wedded or it is the 'Ball and chain' marriage that has lasted for years, all people have their share of highs and lows. This may sound cliché, but every marriage has patterns and lulls of mundanity which are as important as the highs.

The good and the bad are natural to the flow and ebb of life. Periods of boredom, stress, poor c communication, and misunderstandings are all part of the course. And it is true to say 'Marriage takes work and commitment.' Every spouse has to work to make the marriage a beautiful place to be. However, the work done in marriages is not like cleaning trash and getting complete makeovers. The effort that couples put into successful marriages (functional happy and fulfilling relationships) is therapeutic and fulfilling.

What's the secret to a long and happy marriage? It's not grand romantic gestures. The trick is establishing healthy habits and doing those little things day after day, year after year. I asked relationship therapists what the happiest couples say or do that gives the relationship the power to stay. Here is what they told me:

- **They make a point to connect every day**

Couples who are in it for the long haul find little ways to stay physically and emotionally connected, even on the busy days. That might mean going in for a gentle, long hug, listening attentively while your partner is venting (not looking at your phone, *ahem*) or offering words of affirmation and encouragement.

"Emotional connection is the glue in our relationships," marriage and family therapist Jennifer Chappell Marsh told HuffPost. "Over time, these small interactions build into a deep sense of trust and intimacy that keep couples happy and together."

- **They set aside time to check in with each other regularly**

When life gets hectic, couples often switch into autopilot and start going through the motions rather than being intentional about nurturing the relationship. Long-lasting couples, however, make it a point to regularly schedule opportunities to stop, slow down and check in with each other. It might be a quick nightly catch-up session before bed or a more in-depth yearly sit-down conversation.

"Planned check-ins are times when both are mentally prepared to provide each other the space they need to explore, resolve and plan," marriage and family therapist Spencer Northey said. "One couple I know even has an annual 'State of the Union Conference,' where they rent a hotel room and have a 'conference' at the hotel bar to check in and make plans for the coming year."

- **They know how to say sorry and mean it**

"In big or small ways, partners step on each other's

toes all the time," said psychologist Ryan Howes. "Having the humility and maturity to recognize your role in your partner's pain is essential for a long-term relationship."

And, for the record: "Sorry your feelings were hurt" is a half-assed attempt. Instead, aim for an apology that expresses empathy for your partner, takes responsibility for your wrongdoings and shows that you're working to change the behavior.

Howes' suggested that "I see that you're hurt, and it kills me to see you in this pain. I take full responsibility for my part in this, and I'm taking these steps to make sure it doesn't happen again."

• **And they don't hold on to grudges**

Mistakes will be made. Fights will be had. It's par for the course in any relationship. But couples who go the distance don't hold grudges and let resentments fester. They discuss it, work through it and move forward.

"They understand that mistakes are lessons learned and not reasons to shame or punish each other," psychologist and sex therapist Janet Brito said. "When mistakes occur, they are certain that they are still loved and valued."

Spouses who don't hold past transgressions over the other's head are better equipped to handle future conflicts maturely, Howes said.

"Some folks seem to be grievance collectors, who hold on to every relational sin from their partner and wheel them out for the big arguments, especially if they're losing," he said. "'You forgot my birthday 17 years ago' or 'you made me pay for our third date' are grabs at power and rarely result in a constructive conversation. The healthiest couples express how they feel if and when they've been hurt, they do what they can to make sure it doesn't reoccur, they accept the apology, and then they work hard to let go and live in the present."

- **They find little ways to show they are thinking of each other**

Take some time to remind your partner why you love and appreciate them. Longtime couples are in the habit of regularly expressing how much they mean to each other. It doesn't need to be some vast, romantic overture either. It might mean shooting them a text during the workday to thank them for packing you a tasty lunch or picking up a bottle of the wine they were raving about on your honeymoon.

"It could be something you saw that reminded you of them, or you remembered a shared experience that made you smile and wanted to let them know," therapist Juan Olmedo said. "The key is that it be spontaneous: Even an unexpected text message can brighten their day. And no reciprocation is needed. It's just about telling them that you were thinking about them."

- **They communicate about the fun stuff *and* the not-so-fun stuff**

Talking about the positive things in your life — an exciting job offer, the trip you're planning with your best friends — is easy. Talking about the less glamorous — your crippling anxiety disorder, the dissatisfaction you're feeling in your sex life — can be decidedly less fun but essential nevertheless. It's often these more robust conversations that bring you two closer.

"Couples who stay together have uncomfortable conversations where they share difficult emotions," Chappell Marsh said. "When couples feel their expression of distress is seen and heard, their bond strengthens, they become more resilient and their capacity for overall happiness increases."

- **They accept each other's friends and family, imperfections and all**

Maybe your husband's high school buddy is a significant story-topper, and it gets on your nerves. Or perhaps it irks you that your mother-in-law pulls you aside at every family gathering to ask if you're pregnant yet. Even the happiest couples occasionally get annoyed with their partner's friends and family. It's unavoidable. But these couples also recognize that if the person is vital to their partner, it's probably best to smile and suck it up. (Note that the grin-and-bear-it approach may not be appropriate if the friend or relative in question is a toxic person.)

"They make efforts to get to know the most important people in each other's lives," Brito said. "Instead of criticizing each other's loved ones, they focus on their strengths and similarities, and find ways to cultivate a bond, especially if this is important to their partner."

- **In a healthy and happy relationship, couples talk openly and freely**

They understand that their information and message is safe and well receipted. In the initial stages of a relationship, couples can talk about almost everything without worrying about being judged or misinterpreted. Ones they settle in a marriage, communication becomes tougher as the spouses seek to communicate in a respectful yet fun way. Couples in good relationships are comfortable when voicing their worries showing their feelings when problems arise and also express gratitude when things work out. Open and good relationships involve people who talk respectfully to one another without using the accusatory tone with hurtful and insulting things. Everyone listens attentively and ensures that they understand the message that the other person is putting across, verbally and non-verbally. Couples that apply good communication skills show empathy and do not interrupt the other person while trying to prove that the opinions are wrong. At the end of a good conversation, every person feels that their needs have been acknowledged and understood. Good conversations lead to positivity.

- **They make an effort to understand their partner's perspective, even when they don't agree**

Listening to your partner is essential in any relationship, but it's only half the battle. Long-lasting couples hear each other out and then show that they genuinely understand the other's point of view.

"We all have a fundamental need for understanding, so it's crucial to find ways to tell your partner that you understand what she or he is trying to convey, even if you don't agree," Olmedo said. "Being able to say, 'I get what you're saying,' or 'I can see why that matters to you,' can set the stage for you to get your chance to feel heard. Being genuine here is critical."

- **They celebrate their differences, not just their similarities**

At the beginning of a relationship, it may seem like you

and your partner have so much in common: You're both introverts who love hiking on the weekends, chowing down on Korean barbecue and watching Pixar movies. But as time wears on, it becomes clear that, although you may be similar in some ways, you're not the same person. Longtime couples can recognize that these differences keep things interesting and help you both grow.

"Some couples have the unrealistic expectation that they'll enjoy all the same hobbies, have the same opinions and beliefs, and react to life with the same emotions. When they don't, they can feel alone or even abandoned," Howes said. "The healthiest couples can appreciate their partner's different tastes and responses and react to them with curiosity instead of scorn. 'What? Do you like that candidate? I'm so curious why that is because I have exactly the opposite reaction. Tell me more.'"

- **They don't make assumptions about their partner's feelings — they ask**

In the heat of an argument, it's easy to jump to conclusions about what your partner is thinking or feeling. But successful longtime couples can focus on the context of the disagreement at hand, instead of making sweeping generalizations.

"Instead of making broad conclusions about a situation, they inquire about the circumstances and setting, to consider all angles," Brito said. "They don't assume what the other person is feeling but are curious to inquire and are prepared to listen without judgment."

Often, couples who don't know how to argue terminate their arguments prematurely because they're too frustrated or heated to resolve them appropriately. But if you don't come to some resolution — even a temporary one — how can you ever move forward?

"Even though arguments are challenging, you've got to stick with it to find the compromise or solution that you both can live with," Howes said. "I've known couples who never seem to get to the point of resolution with their arguments, and this has a toxic effect on the relationship.

A survey conducted on couples in marriages that had lasted for more than 15 years revealed different basic tips that ensured their success. Below are six tips that were common in almost all the couples:

- **Independence**

One of the aspects that the couples rated as really important for the success of the marriage were Independence. Everyone must first have their happiness before seeking happiness in a relationship. Having that in mind, every spouse must take time by themselves, enjoy their hobbies, and pursue their desires. Spend some time apart; it will help everyone reestablish their sense of self and check their progress. You should remember that absence makes the heart grow fonder. Too much dependency makes one unable to move forward. Independence will keep the conversation fresh in the marriage, and everyone will be more attractive to their partner.

- **Good listening**

Every spouse should work on their listening skills. Men tend to complain that women are annoying because they talk too much and in some cases, the talk is not constructive. They fail to realize that for many women, all that matters is a listening ear. Men need to listen to women and women too need to work on active listening. One should remember that hearing and listening differ. Hearing involves the years while listening entails the heart. Before any person talks, they should listen. Listen and listen some more.

- **Agree to disagree**

Being in a good relationship does not mean that everybody agrees on everything. Many of the couples revealed that they have different attitudes, belief systems, and opinions. They have opposing opinions on some major areas of life. Every couple should have a level of disagreement to maintain balance. As such, every loving couple should agree to disagree and even seek the sense of humor their point of disagreement.

- **Communicate**

In marriage, communication involves identifying the love language of each other. Every individual has a different way of communicating love to their spouse. When one understands the hobbies and preferences of their partner, they will understand the metaphors they use to communicate love. Some people prefer to show rather than speak love. Others prefer to show it by doing favors such as making dinner, picking the children from school, et cetera. Some people prefer to write letters and leave notes for their partners while others prefer physical affection. Couples fail to pay much attention to the language of love thinking that it is a small matter; however, understanding love language is essential.

- **Acceptance**

Acceptance is essential for the success of a marriage. Lack of acceptance is often attributed to spouses who nag. Every spouse should remember that he or she married their partner for who he/she was then and who they are now. Even if the partners change, we should accept them for who they are before we even try to change them. Couples should not focus their arguments on the weaknesses of each other, and when one wishes to correct the other, they should apply tactfulness. Spouses should complement each other and acknowledge their positive attributes daily. This will encourage everybody to stay on the positive side and increase acceptance.

- **Never take each other for granted**

When couples get comfortable in marriage, they tend to take each other for granted. This is one of the most toxic pathogens in marriage. Getting comfortable makes people forget important things including communication. It is human to get comfortable with what they know, but in marriage, couples should not be in a state where they take each other for granted. Every spouse should pledge to respect their partner no matter what. Avoid assumptions, maintain good and open communication, and show love indefinitely.

Chapter 5: Mindful Habits

Make communication strong by sharing healthy habits with your couple. You can do that by coming up with a list of healthy habits in everyday life.

Change your focus. A great way to do this is mindfulness, a non-judgmental presence at the moment. Mindfulness will control those wild running horses; studies show that meditation can reduce cognitive and emotional and bias.

Common practices of healthy couples

"What makes a relationship healthy?" It can be challenging to spot the signs when you're enjoying mind-blowing sex, handmade cards, and romantic dinners. I took a look back at the things I have done (and had done to me) to present you with the mindful practices of healthy couples.

- **You use sex to connect, not to fill a void**

As someone who has tried to find happiness externally in the past, I was never truly aware of why I craved for affection. I have since learned that it is crucial to understand why you need affection and when you need it. Do not be brainwashed and think that having good sex will make you feel validated or address underlying challenges. That needs to be worked out with a coach or therapist, not in our sleeping room.

- **You choose to see the best, not the worst**

We choose where we want to place our attention. And as the saying goes, where attention goes, energy flows. In every situation you have two options:

✓ You can nitpick and use that as an excuse to end the relationship, or

✓ You can choose to appreciate what's good about your significant other.

What are the things that make you love and appreciate your partner? Take a trip down memory lane and remember the funny jokes, hikes, and adventures. This isn't to say you should deny reality, but it's a tool to help you work on the relationship from a place of love rather than fear.

Ultimately, if you look for what he does wrong, you can always find something. If you look for what he does right, you can find something, too. It all depends on what you want to look for. Happy couples accentuate the positive.

- **You see things in the present rather than generalizing patterns**

In a healthy relationship, each person avoids making grandiose statements like "You always..." or "You never..." One instance of doing something that you don't like doesn't define your partner or his behavior throughout the relationship. It's easy for us to want to lump things into patterns, but when you've put an issue to rest, mass generalizations open up old wounds. Treat each instance as a unique event unless you're sure you want to end it.

- **You take responsibility for your growth rather than using the relationship as an excuse to avoid growth**

In a healthy relationship, you take space to pursue a life outside of your partner. After all, he signed on for a partner, not a groupie. In an unhealthy relationship, you define yourself through that union, losing touch with your authentic self. Relationships are spiritual assignments, helping us to evolve into who we're meant to be. When the relationship gets in the way of that, it's time to reevaluate your situation.

- **You communicate what you want instead of what you don't want**

There's a difference between a complaint and a constructive comment. In a healthy relationship, you communicate what you want. For example, it's much more humane to say "I want us to spend time with my family" rather than saying "We spend too much time with your family and not enough with mine." Your positive approach will help put your partner at ease rather than signaling that he should prepare for war.

- **You're open and honest instead of passive-aggressive**

Saying "whatever you want" may squash a problem now, but it creates a pattern of apathy and resentment. In a healthy relationship, you take responsibility for your decisions and healthily communicate them.

- **You show love every day, not only on special occasions**

I once dated a guy who felt that saying "I love you" often would cheapen its meaning. He preferred to save it for special occasions. A healthy relationship is based on a pattern of positive connection, creating intimacy and positive expression. Each party acknowledges and recognizes the other daily. It does not have to be elaborate, but it does have to be sincere, for example,

"You are a wonderful friend." In a healthy relationship, love is expressed with gestures, acts, and words.

- **You spend time together**

Quality time together connects both people. It does not have to be formal. For many people, intimacy is developed through the conscious connection. For example, reading the newspaper at the same time, exercising together, or sharing your morning routine. It is about quality time, not the amount of time. Someone can be great on paper, but without those little moments each day, his or her resume does not hold water.

- **You don't take all his choices personally**

I once argued with my partner over his lifestyle choices, believing that he needed to address his love of cigarettes, pizza, and burgers for us to be a happy couple. As much as I liked to rationalize my arguments; the truth is that he is the one who had to deal with the effects, not me. Things are only your problem when you make them your problem. And while it is your choice to accept his life decisions and choose whether or not you can live with them, it is vital to remember not to take them on a personal level.

While there are many methods to detect an unhealthy relationship, it comes down to connecting with yourself. Are you your authentic self in this relationship? Are you making heart-centered decisions? A healthy love should leave you feeling comfortable, whereas unhealthy love leaves you feeling disconnected and drained.

Chapter 6: Appreciating and Accepting your Partner

You should make it a habit to accept your partners for who they are. Learn how to appreciate and take your partner for what he or she is by not judging your partner. In a relationship between two people who are bound by love, in the beginning, one's partner is transformed into a picture of human perfection. As time goes by the perfection wears off, and each partner discovers how compatible they are, there is at least one thing that each partner dislikes of the other partner. Each partner has a behavior, habit or personal trait that annoys or disappoints the other partner.

As the love story of the two partners goes ahead, they fall in love very much with each other, but their quirks may become a reason for perpetual conflict at home. These failures may often make the other partner feel disappointed and even may end up causing contempt, for the other partner. This may lead to a partner wanting the other partner to change a specific behavior; this may cause a serious feud between the two partners that may end up causing a rift between them. That may also hinder their communication in the committed relationship. For this to work, it is simple, each partner needs to accept that their partner is never going to change and the only way to beat this is by accepting your partner for who they are in every aspect.

Tips on how to accept your partner for who they are in a committed relationship

- **Respecting your partners' beliefs and acknowledging their opinions.**

In a relationship, you don't need to have the same

opinions or subscribe to similar beliefs with that of your partner all the time. You two are unique individuals, who are entitled to their definition of and reaction towards a situation in the environment around you. To accept your partner for who they are means acknowledging that you two will always disagree on several issues, but that doesn't mean that there is a need for an unhealthy reaction such as violence.

- **Accept your partners' imperfections while embracing their flaws.**

You need to accept your partner's significant emotional and physical weaknesses. For example, when your partner is more talented than you or they do not share your level of confidence when it comes to socializing. A partner needs to accept the other imperfection, and all these can be learned, is a matter of time. Accepting your partners' flaws does not mean that you let them hurt you because you still have hope in your partner that he/she will change someday. If a relationship reaches this point it can be toxic and hazardous that should not be tolerated at all.

- **Never force your partner to change to be better.**

It is very unfair for a partner to force the other partner to change the way of living their life. This is because we are unique individuals who are guided by different beliefs and also unique individuals who follow different paths in life. As a couple, you need to accept these differences, so long as their decisions and lifestyle will not hurt the other partner in the relationship. Respect and patience are all that is needed to deal with this, as they will grow up to becoming better persons with time.

- **Knowing your partners' story and what motivates them**

In some instances, one will never understand why they do what they do. With time some decisions will be confusing for one partner that may lead to the partner to question their sanity; this is because they do not agree with how the other partner wants things to be done. In this case, how do you deal with such a situation? One needs to know where his or her partner is coming from and the underlying reasons that made him or her what they are currently. You need to listen and know their story, and you also need to respect the lessons life has taught them. Trust is also essential in this situation, trust your partner for them to do the right thing not just because you love and care about them, trust them because you believe in their capabilities in life.

- **Do not compare your partner with other people from your past.**

You should never compare your current partner to your past love life or with the people you have met in the past. To some partner, this will only be a deal-breaker that may lead to them being hurt and worried. Love your partner for who they are now and please do not go looking for more. You should move on from your past and accept your partner in your present life. If this cannot be the case, then you do not deserve their everlasting love.

- **Love your partner for who they are from the inside**

You should ask yourself what made you fall in love with your partner in the first place? I hope it is what was inside them, their personality, their soul and heart, their smile and the little things that make them unique to you. As we all know that love is not blind it helps us to see what we have been missing in our love life: a special soul, a special heart, a unique soul and an unusual love that brings with it sincere and genuine joy and happiness in our days.

- **Being patient with your partner and giving them time to grow**

For a relationship to last, maturity makes a big difference in that relationship. In some relationship couples do not share the same level of experience and understanding; this may be caused by a gap in terms of their age difference. Despite your relationship being compatible as you may believe, sometimes a gap in age or difference in maturity can affect your relationship in a negative way. For you like the older person in the relationship and more experienced, you have the responsibility to wait for them to grow. You need to guide them through this passage and the learning process. Patience is necessary when guiding them to be the best person your partner was meant to be.

- **Being proud of your partner and show them you mean it**

Always be proud of your partner for what they have accomplished in their life and what they have become. Being aware of their past and struggles that they have faced, appreciate them and compliment them of what they have achieved, a job well done. The only acceptable way to show your partner that you accept them for who and what they are in a committed relationship is for you to be happy about the goals they have achieved and show to everyone that you are proud of your partners' achievements. Tell your partner that they are perfect in their imperfect ways that will be the sweetest and ideal act to show love to your partner.

Appreciating your partner in a relationship

After you have accepted your partner for who they are in a relationship, you should then appreciate your partner in a committed relationship. Being appreciative to your partner is one of the most beneficial activities you can do for your relationship. Appreciating your partner is fun and enriching. Verbal appreciation shows how much you adore your partner and shows you are committed to the relationship. It also shows that their efforts are appreciated no matter how small they may seem to be.

Showing value in a relationship is critical; this allows one to know where they stand in a relationship and also what they mean to you. When a partner in a relationship is dedicated, and yet they do not know how valuable they are to that relationship. This changes how that person operates and function in that union. When you do not show value to your partner, and they believe so, the other partner tends to devalue the relationship.

Here are the reasons why you should show your partner you appreciate them:

- It makes it easier for your partner to show you that they appreciate you also.

You need to show that you appreciate someone first before you are welcomed too. By doing so, it makes it easier for your partner to show appreciation to you also. The main reason as to why people tend to withhold recognition is that they do not feel recognized in the first place.

- Makes your partner feel happy

Most people tend to feel happy when they do things for other people. They derive happiness by them being generous in giving or offering services to other people. This may change when this type of people do not get any sign of appreciation of what they are doing. They become disgruntled about doing so. Some act, do not need any payment, but by just simply telling them that you appreciate their act of kindness and their efforts, this makes them feel happy.

- Being appreciated makes them feel loved

Most often, people feel that the person they love does not love them back the same way they love them. You love your partner because of what you feel about them, so when you appreciate them, you are telling them how much you love them back.

- It makes your partner feel special

This makes a person in a relationship feel honored, treasured and special. You are telling your partner how much you mean to them and how important they are in that relationship. By doing so, your relationship will be based on a special ground that will make it stronger than ever.

- It shows that you respect your partner

Respect plays a bigger role in the success of a relationship. With no respect, a relationship is doomed to fail.

- It is a sign that you are grateful for what they do for you

When a partner receives appreciation from you, it motivates them to keep doing it. By them being motivated it creates a kind of consistency in the action they do, and nothing provides consistency like recognition.

Signs showing that your partner is not feeling appreciated in a relationship

1. Your partner is quicker to argue

2. Your partner is often sad.

3. Having a feeling of growing distance between the two of you.

4. Your partner becomes more quiet than usual

5. Your partner becomes more emotional than before

6. When your partner stops doing things they are used to do.

Naturally, when you put hard work into something, it is always a great thing to get a pat on the back for the efforts you have put. When you are more appreciative to your partner in a relationship and also being grateful for the contribution, your partner brings in your life, the happier the two of you will be as couples. Always remember to make appreciating to your partner as the priority.

Ways of showing your partner that you appreciate them

1. Expressing love to your partner often. Good

relationships are those that evolve when it comes to love, appreciating your partner love will never be enough. It is always a consistent thing that needs to be revisited each time you are with your partner.

2. Always spend time together with your partner. Laugh together, be playful together and always have fun while you appreciate each other.

3. Often compliment your partner even on little things. For example "that red dress makes you look vibrant. I love it; my dear."

4. Always acknowledge the things that make you love your partner. -for example their friend or their family.

5. Appreciate your partner for always being there for you, in your ups and challenging moments of your life. Your partner is the person who invests most of their time on you, more than any other person in your life.

6. By appreciating your partner, it shows them that you do not take them for granted in any way.

7. Always thank your partner for the small things that make a big difference in your life -for example ironing your clothes, preparing food for you and washing dishes for you.

8. Paying total attention to your spouse when they are talking to you about any matter that affects you two. Ensure that you make full eye contact when you are having a conversation with your partner, this shows that you are paying full attention and you are serious about the matter.

Importance of showing appreciation to your spouse

- A partner who shows appreciation in a relationship is more committed to the relationship and is more likely to stay in the relationship for long.

- A partner who savors his/her present or past has a greater joy in the relationship than those who do not savor their past or present situations.

- By eliminating positive events mentally, one can spur appreciation. This type of strategy helps one to improve their positive emotions and their well-being.

- When a partner attempts to foster appreciation by them comparing themselves with others, it boosts both negative and positive emotions. Always remember to be very cautious when you are drawing comparisons to others in a relationship.

- Being appreciative is not all positive. In some cases, appreciation can lead to lowering one's aspirations. This happens when you draw attention away from future possibilities. So it's always advised to be mindful of a balance between aspiration and appreciation in one's life.

- Gratitude towards your partner is associated with stronger ties in a relationship, greater willingness in the partner to share concerns in the relationship and it also creates a higher level of marital satisfaction.

Replacing judgment with compassion in a relationship

Every person always has a dream to be in a relationship that they feel entirely free from judgment and safe.

Sometimes a couple finds themselves regularly clashing, judging one another for their poor actions or decisions. This constant argument between them only cause division or forms a larger wedge space between them, instead of creating intimacy and love between them. For you to stop judging your partner, take time and eliminate the judgmental thought that you have in your mind and instead replace it with a sense of gratitude that your partner is always there for you, for better or for worse.

Create a feeling of compassion for your partner instead of the judgmental thought. For example, when your spouse arrives late home from work, instead of negative, judgmental views about them, you need to frame your thoughts into compassion for him/her, for having a long day at work.

This kind of reaction is called Radical Acceptance. Radical Acceptance is powerful, beautiful and most importantly transformative practice. Most importantly you need to commit to the intention and to merely be aware of when you are judgmental to your partner, and the need to call yourself out appropriately.

Finally, it is vital to accept and appreciate your partner as they are and for what they bring in your life. Always focus on the positives in your relationship; this will create a stronger bond between couples. Challenges in the relationship always arise, but the best way for the two of you to deal with the problems is both you to have a candid and sincere conversation about the negatives in your relationship. This will allow both of you to come up with an agreement and how to deal with the situation amicably.

By couples accepting and appreciating each other,

it will create a good environment for the couple to communicate more openly without holding anything back.

Chapter 7: The Ego Monster

Ego is the most dangerous thing in relationships; eliminate your ego to get a neutral point of view.

The term ego refers to when a partner in a relationship feels the entitlement of things to be done their way. People develop ego because they think they are superior to others. In a love relationship, when you turn and let your ego to make crucial decisions in your relationship rather than your spirit, this will lead to manipulation as a means to give and receive love. This is because the ego does not have any relationship skill. Whenever you try to protect yourself, ego resorts to fighting, sarcasm, depression, aggression, intolerance, blame, resentment, distrust, frustration, rude gestures and self-doubt.

Choices that we make out of our ego end up being the very obstacle to our relationship and love life. This, in turn, ends up being ego battleships instead of the committed relationship between two persons.

For natural love in a relationship, there is no need for manipulation to receive or give love. One's spirit loves, and it is capable of loving with no conditions or expectations. Our spirits also utilize the relationship skills of wisdom, acceptance, forgiveness, apologizing, being creative, being responsible, understanding and being discerning.

Signs of egoism in a relationship

- **Losing yourself.** This happens when one gives up their desires, hobbies, values, and even, at times, family and friends to please another individual. By doing so, we allow the ego to get love. You might think that the only way to get love from another person is by you to alter yourself into something that the other person wants; this is ego operating. The more you pretend to be something that you are not, the less loved you will feel. Hence, approval becoming the only hurdle in you receiving the love.

- **Constant judgment and criticism.** When you act out of your ego, you may think that the best way to love someone is by changing them, the effort of love becomes the need for control.

- **A partner that needs to be always right.** When one allows their ego to be in control of their feelings and in the way of love, this individual will always choose themselves, and they will always feel the need to be right above anyone else even their spouse.

- **A partner that needs to be always in control.** This occurs when a partner feels the need to have overwhelming control over the other partner in a relationship. You may end up putting your own needs above the needs of the other person. This allows one partner to choose what and how they believe things should be done over love.

- **Shutting down your partner in the middle of a conversation.** Allowing ego to take control makes one not to respect the opinions or views of the other person. Ego will make you feel the need to shut down the opinion of your partner especially if their opinion differs with your opinion. This is the worse level of intolerance in a committed relationship.

- **A partner will refuse to talk about some specific topics in life.** A partner with a strong ego will tend to avoid discussion of topics that they do not want. The need for a partner to decide what is acceptable and that which is not acceptable is an act of one partner; this should not be the case because of the concept of two as a couple, not one.

- **A partner will refuse or hold back to solve a misunderstanding.** People with strong ego will tend to stay angry in an argument for a long time, and this does not bother them at all. They do not feel the importance of solving the matter as soon as possible. Extreme ego tends to make a decision that is against the wishes of the person they love.

How ego can kill a relationship

One of the biggest challenges we have in our relationships is that most people get into a relationship to get something they desire. This kind of people tends to find someone who will make them feel good according to their desire. Naturally, a relationship is a place where you go to give, and not a place where you go to take.

You should accept and give importance to others rather than allowing ego to consume you and ignore the importance of the other partner in a relationship. Every human being is different and so do their opinions differ. It is difficult to accept the opinions of others or make a compromise on them. In a relationship, if you do not do so, this will kill a relationship. Having self-respect is ideal for all, when you give importance to your partner, appropriately attend to him/her and show them the affection that is needed. Attitude is a factor that can help in solving a problem in a damaging relationship.

The most important part of interaction is the ability

to listen to other person views first before reacting. When a partner has filled themselves with ego, during an interaction it will be difficult for them to listen to the other partner; this is because ego has made them feel superior to their partner.

One's ego can ruin a conversation with your spouse

In most cases people allow their pride to take over a conversation. You may think that you are too smart to even listen to the other person. We may also think that we are better than the other person and we have nothing more to learn from them. When you close yourself from listening to other people, you are doomed; this is because you stop learning. For you to eliminate this listening barrier, you have to be more open-minded, by learning from other people and also by listening to other people views and opinions. It costs you nothing by just listening; you do not need to agree with everything that is said.

Signs showing that ego is destroying your relationship

- Others are better than you. Ask yourself are you playing the victim card in your relationship? Are you comparing yourself to your partner? Do you put yourself down to get a rise? You will realize that ego will always partake in negative reinforcement rather than in positives reinforcement. If you are doing the above habits, you need to step back and reexamine your relationship.

- Jealousy. This is a monster that provides the greatest platform of drama in a relationship. Ego thrives well in lack of self-acceptance and self-worth.

When you allow jealousy to engulf your relationship you are allowing jealousy to create the highest form of toxic energy in your relationship. If you are in an abusive relationship, ego will make you maintain this type of relationship through jealousies. If your partner is making you question the relationship, then you need to raise the red flag to step back and be sincere with the kind of abusive relationship you are in.

- Having a fear of rejection. This kind of fear makes you not achieve any goal that you had set, and by doing so, you are doing injustice to your relationship. Ego creates this fear in a person, instead of listening to the voice of ego and fear, you need to shift your perception from the ego's anxiety and to nag to a constructive way to gain self-confidence that you will achieve whatever you had set no matter what. Remember that your ego thrives when you have negative self-talk. An intimate relationship is built upon mutual acceptance and admiration. When you feel rejection to your partner, then it's time for you to analyze your commitment with your partner.

- Feeling that you must have the last word. Turning everything in a relationship to be a one-man play, this is a cause of ego in a relationship. When you realize that you and your partner have excessive discussions without asking about the other, well that is a sign that you are in an ego-driven relationship. Ego plays a crucial role in ensuring that you do not achieve complete happiness and peace. Ego also creates a scenario that does not naturally exist, for example when you find yourself to be always having the last say on everything, it is time for you to step back and find the root cause.

- Constant blaming. This happens when you find yourself always blaming your partner for everything. You need to know that in a relationship it is about a couple two people and not one person. This is caused by our ego in a relationship. Ego is controlling your relationship and use manipulation to make it work. Ego loves to criticize and blame. When one does not take responsibility for their actions in a relationship, ego will use this to project to another negative situation.

How to control your ego and improve your relationship

The following techniques can help you learn how to let go of your ego:

- **Practicing letting go and forgiveness.** One of the most powerful tools that will help you in letting go of your ego is to practice forgiveness. You need to learn how to forgive people who hurt you and also learn how to forgive yourself. By forgiving, you will be able to accept, let go and keep moving forward to achieve your set goal. Forgiveness will allow your soul to remove the negativity in our inner being and allow a new wave of happiness in our soul.

- **Practicing being open and honest.** One of the most important statements that I know we have all come across in our day to day routine is "The truth will set us free." Holding onto the truth will suppress your emotions that will make you develop depression and anxiety. Being honest will always provide you with unconditional freedom for you to be connected with yourself instead of you trying to be something that you are naturally not. Learn to say No to the things or matters that do not add value to your life, accept and open your arms to things that bring positive impact in your life.

- **Learn to Surrender Your Need to be always in Control.** When you let your ego control your love relationship, it will always make you conform to things or Statue that is not part of your natural being. By doing so, you do things that you are not used to doing, and when you lose one of the things that you have created to make yourself what you want, you will realize that all the other things that you identify yourself with will fall like dominos and this will lead to you losing your happiness. Do what makes you happy as a person, be curious and be a risk taker. Take a challenge every day and do something that scares you and notices that you will start to feel happy in the small things that you do.

- **Having silent moments to yourself and enjoy it.** Create a daily routine that reminds you of how special you are and why it is beautiful for you to be yourself. In the same daily routine perform an act of self-love and enjoy doing it. Five minutes every day for you to be alone and in silence. Sometimes in silence, you may find answers that in noise or voices can never find.

- **By practicing gratitude.** Create time for yourself every day for you to think about all the experiences, lessons and mistakes that you have achieved in your day to day life and be thankful to all those. In life, it is about the challenges we face and how we react to them that makes us succeed and be happy in life. People who are always appreciative tend to feel more loved and compassion, compared to people who are consistently not grateful of any deed since they live in self-denial. This is a breeding ground for the ego to thrive and other negative thoughts. Showing appreciation will also show you the beauty of life.

The battle of love versus ego

As human beings, we all have an ego within us. All we need to do is to learn to control our ego and not to let it control our lives. Letting your ego go unchecked can cause tremendous turmoil in your life especially with our closest and intimate relationships. Having negative emotions, for example, fear, jealousy, and anger are all products of ego. We all have two opposing forces that battle against each other in our inner being. In a battle, each side always has its agenda, idea, and suggestions. The forces are always opposite one another. These two forces in us are the force of Ego and the force of Love. It is upon you to choose which one will control or govern your life.

How the battle unfolds

1. **The force of ego.** This kind of force makes you decide with the help of your ego rather than your spirits. The negative thing about the force of ego is that it has no any relationship skill. Instead, it uses manipulation to receive love and give love. The force of ego makes one have fear, that loving will result from hurting, and it also creates a fear that if you love so much, you will abandon the concept of ego, that is self-protection and separation. Ego Love is a mirror of the desire and need of the lover and not the loved one. This kind of love only rests on the mercy of one partner, the partner that is being manipulative to receive the love. It asks them to be something that they cannot possibly be, that

is what you want them to be, rather than what they are. This practice leads to disappointment and disillusionment that will lead to resentment. All in all the Genesis of all these things will lead to breaking up of a relationship.

2. **Force of love.** This is a force that drives us towards good deeds. It ensures one to be always sensitive and kind at all times. It admonishes you when you are neglectful and unkind to your partner or people close to you. In this kind of love, there are no demands that are placed to the other partner compared to the Ego Love. This is because in this Love force there are no demands. With no demands on this kind of love, there are no expectations from any party. This kind of love takes ego out of our hearts; it controls every aspect of our life and every move that we make, hence creating beauty and joy wherever we go.

How you can deal with a person with a huge ego

1. Do not be afraid to be a little rude to someone you know has a big ego.

2. Try not to make any sense out of their behavior; this is because someone with a huge ego tends not to make any sense.

3. When they do not even agree with you on normal facts, please just don't try to argue with them.

4. When you are in a conversation with someone with a huge ego, talk facts and not emotions.

5. There is a need to cut some phrases from your speech, for example, do not try sentences with: I feel..., I think..., I just.... and I sort of...... This is

because such phrases will automatically make you sound less superior to them.

6. At the start of any conversation with someone with a huge ego, it is advisable for you to adjust your attitude so as you are not expecting a crappy talk.

7. Always do not take it personally if they tend to use vulgar language or abuse you.

Chapter 8: Love Unconditionally

The secret to having everything is not expecting anything. The concept of unconditional love in an intimate relationship is a noble course. We all want to be loved as we are and for what we are. You should love a person for who they are their personality traits and their ideologies. Without any conditions made, one would be able to bestow unconditional love to their partners.

Unconditional love comes with caring about the happiness of another person with no concerns of how it will benefit you as a person. This kind of love is similar to those who are involved in a maternal love or romantic love; this is connected or linked to the brains reward system. It shows that unconditional love is rewarding without receiving something in return.

Romantic unconditional love

This kind of love is based on whether adults who are involved in that relationship can also show each other this type of unconditional love. In this relationship you need to feel safe; it is sensible that you need to feel as though the other person will not leave you based on a whim. One needs to be assured that the other person is committed to loving them unconditionally despite what the future will bring. In romantic unconditional love, for love to continue existing, there should be mutual respect between the couple, not an attitude of your partner. In this case, you will put up with your partners' behavior and stick to them no matter what they do.

Positive unconditional love

In this kind of love, unconditional love does not mean that you always give people what they want or always accepting what they do, at the mercy of your personal needs. This is a kind of mature love that you treat the person that you love with respect while even maintaining your boundaries and protecting oneself. You recognize your main purpose; in the face of your partners' behavior, you pass your message with respect and love. This comes with being attuned and attentive, even while you set your boundaries you still mind the request of your partner and honoring them without hurting yourself.

This requires you not being dismissive and harsh as this will lead to no compromises. Communicating to your partner where you stand and your view on a certain issue, so that both of you can work out the best solution.

How to love unconditionally

This means that the couple should set their eyes on what keeps them together.

- **Embracing every moment you spend together.** Life is filled with ups and downs in a relationship. You are required to accommodate every aspect of your partners' life including the ups and downs. No love is perfect; the sad part of it is as important as the good part of it.

- **Do not surrender at the site of imperfection.** Naturally, no one is perfect, that also applies to your partner he/she make mistakes. You both have obsessions, particularities, flaws, and different views. Even if your partner is not perfect, it doesn't mean he/she is not the right person for you. People with most easy-going attitudes also have quirks. You need to understand and learn that not you or your partner is perfect, but you both need to work things out to make it work for both of you.

- **Always strive to work through hard times.** Endurance, during your hard times, is very crucial to unconditional love. Do not allow the unfavorable and dark conditions fool you that you cannot be in the relationship that may lead you to give up. Always have the strength and right mentality to believe that your love is worth fighting for and work through the obstacles together. In the end, you come out victorious, and your relationship will come out stronger than ever.

- **Having mutual respect and striking a balance.** One should always work out a formula to divvy up responsibilities, chores, and tasks in a relationship. By doing so, you will have figured out a balance in your relationship. Relationships will always involve the aspect of giving and taking, hence no need to create a feeling of resentment in either one of the couple. You should make compromises for your partner and also allow your partner to make compromises for you; this will create Respect between the two of you.

- **Create a feeling of happiness that you and your partner deserve.** This is the most crucial aspect of unconditional love that is both of you deserve to be happy. No one would ever suggest being in a relationship that they feel they are unhappy. Having a belief that you and your partner deserve to be happy, will put you in the right direction. Some trials and tribulations come with putting together two different lives into one, these trials and tribulations need not be ignored but to be accepted wholeheartedly. Unconditional love will make your stay in that relationship and make it work to the best of your abilities.

How to know that you have found unconditional love

- Being able to freely express each other concerns, even when it feels to be uncomfortable.

- When you admit your failings, your partner will not judge you or shame you. Instead, they will hold your hand through recovery.

- When one gets vulnerable, the partner will respond with empathy and encourage the partner while trying to allay any fears.

- Forgiving each other freely with no conditions. Forgiving and completely forgetting.

- When you wrong your partner, you will actively pursue restitution and act on rebuilding your lost trust to your partner.

- No holding of grudges or pick up arguments over petty issues that can be talked through and be solved amicably. If it reaches a point of arguments, you respect each other and objectively resolve in a healthy resolution.

- When you do not need to prove anything or yourself to your partner

- When your partner sincerely places your needs before their own needs, without any expectations of receiving anything in return.

- Your partner takes time to encourage you and inspires you, for them to bring the best out of you or the best version of you.

- Celebrating each other successes while you appreciate them.

- Having a deep empathy towards your partner.

- Feeling safe when you are around your partner.

- When you both consider communication to be very important.

Unconditional love does not mean you are there no matter what you do

Many people may think from the definition of unconditional love that a person will stay in a relationship with a person no matter what they do. You might think that true love means overlooking all that your partner does and never giving up on them. This kind of myth can be hazardous and misguiding. It has caused very many people to stay in an abusive relationship, without them speaking up on what is happening to them in reality. They pretend everything to be working okay and in the right direction. Whatever your partner does every day affect your life positively or negatively, your emotions and also your feelings and your well-being hence the need of not overlooking your partners' actions in the name of unconditional love.

Unconditional love is not being codependent

Unconditional love means you support your partner no matter what happens to them; this is the contrast of them taking advantage of your love. They should not rely on you to meet all their emotional satisfaction. Nevertheless, everyone is responsible for their happiness. A relationship that is unhealthy, emotional reliance is codependency; this is not unconditional love.

A relationship is codependent when one partner: Relies too much on the other person to feel happy, you lose your identity, or when you no longer think that you are an independent party in the relationship.

Unconditional love is not all about your partner

As a human being, you have your flaws. You are not required to love every single flaw in your partner. Unconditional love means that you dislike a few traits in your partner which is ultimately the nature of human beings. Being in love with every single character of your partner can imply that you are only focusing on the good qualities. You deny yourself the opportunity to believe that your partner could have anything negative about them.

Unconditional love does not mean over-protecting your partner

Fact is that no one would ever wish to see something terrible happening to the people they love. Having a desire to protect your partner is a natural response to the personal relationship we have with our loved ones. Though at times being overprotective might stand in the way of progress. A person would wish to see their partner take steps to improve their livelihood and for them to achieve the goals they have set in life. In the process of them making the steps, the process will be filled with risks and failures. It is with these failures and risks that disappointment and pain will manifest in that journey. By one loving their partner, you should understand that some of this pain can't be avoided and it is even necessary for the pain for them to get to where they want to be in life. So by being overprotective to them, you will hurt them in the process of protecting them so much or even hinder them from achieving the goals they had set.

True unconditional love allows a couple to change and grow as individuals overtime

In a relationship, love is viewed as shared personal values and desires in life. A couple should understand this will change over time. As the couple develops and works together to ensure they are a better couple and also better individuals in the future. The truth is that you are together because you want to support each other by making critical changes. You will want to see your partner grow and improve in their desires. When you notice an emotional distance growing between the two of you, this is because your values and traits do not align with the other person.

Developing at a personal level will help you begin to notice the difference, and this will help each partner to align their desire with the other partner. Unconditional love allows you to be joyful even when your partner is not around; this is because you have grown in person to improve your self-confidence. It makes you understand that you can be independent, even when each one of you is pursuing their desires.

It gives one certain freedom in a relationship. In this freedom, you need to be your person, have some personal time alone, have time to achieve your personal goals and live happily. When you can meet your set goals, you will have a better understanding of yourself. Understanding yourself, knowing yourself and loving yourself allow one to love another person or your partner unconditionally.

Unconditional love is not one -way

When your partner does not love you the same way you love them, it is not unconditional love this is what we call damaging self-sacrifice. You need to hold yourself to the same level that you expect your partner to hold you in and that you should make sure that they adhere to it. This is referred to as mutually supportive, meaning each partner pulls the other up to the healthiest way of loving and not either of the partners tearing one another down. You should consider asking your partner to love you more healthily and respectfully. Love acts reciprocally. This may sound like setting demands, but it understands your self-worth. This is the only way one can improve his/her relationship.

Relationship break down

Human beings are programmed to love conditionally. You love your partner due to his/her unique character traits and qualities. These are the traits that attracted you to them. These are the reasons why you love him/her and not any other person. The tricky part arises when the person you love changes in terms of the personal traits, if they change, at what level is love withdrawn?

True mature love comes with no strings attached. This kind of love is a behavior rather than a feeling. It reaches a point of confusion that leads to breaking down of the intimate relationship. Unconditional love satisfaction should arise from the act of giving it to the other partner, and not from what one will receive in return. When you think of unconditional love as an expression of our kindest being, then it can be maintained even when a relationship does not survive.

An example is when a couple still loves another despite them not being together. When you feel that a relationship is hurting you more, then that relationship is not good for you. It is perfect and advisable for you to feel the unconditional love but say goodbye to the relationship. This kind of love is basic in the goodness and total acceptance of someone; this does not mean that you should tolerate abuse, neglect or other deal breakers. When you first fell in love with your partner, the state at that point can be referred to as unconditional. But do not forget that we live in a conditional world where relationships do come to an end. This is because we all have different needs and choices that we make individually, and these desires and needs do change with time. Ties that completely lack unconditional love are unlikely to survive. Lifestyle and needs do change with time, if you are not ready and willing to see your partner go through a process of change, this could be a reason for the breaking of the relationship for the both of you.

A partner can be more important to the other person when they offer unconditional love in a mature sense. This is possible by one of the partners being mindful of the present situation. When you struggle by doing so, you should practice mindful meditation. Practicing mindful meditation will help you to slow down and be aware of your relationship needs. By doing so, it might also help you to learn how to show yourself the same unconditional love that you are trying to offer to you love partner. When one does not show themselves, unconditional love, first, it will be difficult for them to offer it to their partner.

Conditional love vs. unconditional love

Have you ever asked yourself if there is a difference between conditional love and unconditional love? The answer is yes.

In conditional love, you love someone conditionally; you tend to want your partner to act, look, and think in ways that fit your expectations and paradigms. This kind of love comes from your ego. You tend to hold your partner accountable for your expectations for them to qualify for your affection. In this kind of love, when your partner acts the way you want them to, you express your approval and satisfaction; if they act opposite to what you want them to do, you tend to withhold your expression of acceptance on them, and this is usually expressed in the form of anger. Conditional love polarizes your inner thoughts for you to believe that you are always right and your partner is ever wrong and that your partner should see things your way, not their way. You will always think entirely on the power play and try as much as possible to be in control of everything. This will trigger a defensive reaction from your partner.

When you look at conditional love in the aspect of sexual feelings, you will tend to find someone who will complete you or satisfy you rather than someone who you will share your whole-self with completely. When you act in a way that vastly deviates from your norm or natural expectations or you do something that hurts the people you love or your partner, this emotion can be completely transformed with time to move to the opposite spectrum which is hatred. If you find yourself at this point of hatred, you should step back and re-examine your relationship. Hatred is deeply rooted in fear and can cause real havoc in a relationship; it can be destructive on your emotional, mental, and physical well-being.

Comparing the conditional love to that of unconditional love, you will realize in unconditional love nothing is expected from your partner or the people you love. You will tend to reason with your spirit not as compared to conditional love where you will find yourself reasoning and making a decision based on your ego.

Unconditional love comes to you through the soul level. It starts at the level of self-forgiveness and self-acceptance. It will radiate divine light to your partner and everyone you love. Unconditional love will always have a positive impact on your emotional, physical, mental and spiritual well-being. When you open your heart to receive unconditional love, you will feel radiant and expansive; you will find yourself rising above the limitations of fear, this is because this kind of love is the most powerful force in existence.

Chapter 9: Set Goals for Your Relationship

In this chapter, you are going to learn about creating and setting real relationship goals. By doing so, you will be able to enhance and protect your love and also enhance communication with your partner or your spouse. You should have a reality check, ask yourself how much time do you spend nurturing and improving your love relationship? When you enter into a romantic relationship, you feel that the intoxicating fuel of infatuation will forever power your relationship at the same level. With time, the fuel runs low, and the relationship begins to hobble along on vapors. Some signs of such a point in the relationship are when the couple no longer has long chats getting to know how each other spent their day at work. The couple does not even get free time for them to spend together as it was the norm at the beginning of the relationship.

When it reaches this point, most couples do not know what to do, so they prefer not doing much or anything to revive their connection. How do you enjoy the profound satisfaction that is there in the long term committed relationship?

This can be achieved by understanding the stage of your relationship and setting mutual couple goals. This process will be a success by the commitment to daily actions to meet the best relationship targets for you and your partner or spouse.

What are these couple relationship goals?

Each person has a personal goal for their career, for their development, and self-improvement. As you have individual targets for personal growth, you and your partner can mindfully consider what is best for your relationship, creating and setting relationship goals, how the goals will be, and how both of you are going to achieve them. A committed relationship is an evolving connection which is also very dynamic due to the changes that occur over time. If both partners do not proactively think of what the future in that relationship should look like and how they can grow and evolve together despite the changes. Things might grow apart if the couple does not take drastic action.

These changes in life at a personal level may cause disconnection, unhappiness, and conflict. But all these can be avoided if the couple works together towards a common goal, remaining flexible as life changes arise, by doing so you might be able to protect your bond and enjoy all the benefits of relationship goals.

Relationship goals for couples to nurture and protect their bond

- **Prioritizing your relationship.** By being honest, most people tend to talk big about the importance of their marriage, but when it comes to reality when the rubber meets the road, they are not putting their relationship as the priority. As time passes by you, start taking one another for granted. One gets busy, and they get distracted with their stuff, and they neglect to check the desires of their partners. One should view the relationship as a given, a byproduct of his/her connection to the other person. You should know that a relationship is an entity of its own made up of three blocks that are, there is your partner, there is the relationship, and there is you. Comparing the three, the relationship is the first place that should be prioritized over everything else in your life. So setting the relationship as a goal should be a mutual goal, that both partners embrace it with open arms, as it is the centerpiece or the core of your life. How can you achieve this? Simple by just being committed to it every single day of your life, in all the decision that you make and actions that you take.

- **Creating a couple bubble.** This bubble reinforces the goal of prioritizing relationship by you thinking of "we" rather than "me." This goal tends to be very difficult for most couples; this is caused by the aspect of one viewing themselves as a team first above their independent habits and desires. Apart from the belief of being inter-dependence, that one's feel it is weakening them, in the real sense, it is strengthening you because each person feels cherished and a feeling of being safe is created. For you to achieve this particular goal, you need to make a series of mutual agreements with your partner that reinforces your care and protection of the relationship. This goal also involves you becoming an expert on your partners' needs, fears, and desires, quickly repairing damage to the relationship. By having a reservoir for happy events in your life, these memories counter any difficulties and also act like a rock in times of difficulty.

- **Having daily time for connection.** This is a fundamental daily goal for a couple. You should set time daily for one-on-one time together to reconnect. The most important aspect of this goal is that you can be there in person for your partner. You are focused on each other with no distractions. For couples who work outside the home, this is a very important goal for the couple to set. Make it a habit to do this early in the morning before the workday start or in the evenings before both of you are pulled away to responsibility and chores. You should not take this time to work through conflicts. No, you should take this time to talk, share, embrace and simply enjoy each other's company. The connection time should not be long hours; this should take to about twenty minutes to twenty-five minutes.

- **Communicating to your partner with kindness.** In setting a common couple goal, you must include the ways you communicate with your partner. Avoid using covert words and behaviors that are profoundly wounding; this over time will accumulate enough to cause serious problems in your relationship. One loses trust, mutual respect and finally, the love is lost. One should make it a purpose in their goal to be kind during communication with your partner. Being kind during communication doesn't mean that you are obliged to agree with each other's sentiment.

- **Embracing Vulnerability.** We all have vulnerabilities that we tend to hide from our partners so as they don't think less of us. In a relationship, as intimacy and trust grow, this is the time you should share some of your vulnerabilities with your partner. This will help you find a place of security and safety, where you can offload your baggage in life, and you can, at last, be yourself completely. Having a sense of security and safety with your vulnerabilities is with your partner. By doing this, you can strengthen the bond between you and your spouse. This also fosters a deeper state of intimacy and love. When you treat the vulnerabilities of your partner with dignity, this can heal wounds from a past event and make you feel more confident of who you are. Make it a purpose for you to be completely open, real to each other and vulnerable.

- **Maintaining a satisfying sex life.** Despite you having a greater sex life with your partner at the beginning of your relationship, with time, this will grow to a boring or even burdensome from time to time. This can be avoided by you understanding your partners' needs that are related to sex as well as acknowledging your desires. Men are more visually stimulated and variety as compared to women. For women, they need to feel secure and comfortable with their sex partner for them to be willing to try new things and for them to be sexually adventurous.

- **Always plan to have fun together as a couple.** For a couple, the relationship should be a place of peace and a place to rest from the daily tribulations or your day to day routine. It should provide you with an outlet for enjoying and having fun to the fullest with your partner. Your life has been stressful and serious, with your days spent at work, taking care of your children, carrying out one to another errand and also dealing with daily situations. Your relationship is the place where you can run and have a humble resting opportunity. Try and bring back the early memories you had with your partner when you first met, the amount of time you spent together and the fun you had together. Couples should practice playing a couple of games and having fun together; this increases bonding and communication between the couple and relationship satisfaction. Purpose to create time every week for you and your partner to have fun and enjoy together.

- **Supporting each other's personal goals.** As important as having a couple of bubble relationship goal, it is also important for you and your partner to have personal goals and dreams of your own. By having personal goals as a couple, you should not undermine your connection as a couple. This should strengthen your relationship as each one of you has a unique and promising idea to bring to the relationship. You should both know that the most important person in your life is your spouse or your partner, someone that admires and supports your goals and will always to see you succeed in all your set targets.

- **Having a yearly review.** When you and your spouse have time to set and create common goals, you should also create time to measure the level of success of your efforts. Sit down at the end of the year; discuss each of the goals you had set for your relationship. Ask yourselves the following questions

- How successful have you been in achieving your goals?

- What are the steps you have taken in the past to actualize your goals?

- What are the areas that you need to work on to actualize your common couple desires?

Ensure that you have used this time well to come up with new goals for the coming year, which build on what you had already achieved in the previous year.

Long-term relationship goals

There will always be evolution and changes in your relationship as time goes by and all that you want as a couple is for your love and closeness to withstand the test of time. When you and your partner have real relationship goals that you have set, this will act as a buffer to caution you against the challenges that often come with the changes over time. The cushion or buffer also protects the relationship from being torn down apart. Having set a couple of goals, it encourages you and your partner to set the bar high for your relationship rather than allowing your connection to erode and wither with time.

Here are some ways in which you and your partner will achieve the above common couple goals:

- Ensure that the goals you have both sets make you feel good about yourselves. You can't achieve something opposite of your values. Sharing your couple's goals can be beneficial to others as well as yourselves, as it will act as a powerful bonding experience.

- Having talks as a couple of where you need to be in the next six months to one year. Keep it positive.

- You need to make sure that your personal goals are in line with your couple relationship goals. The alignment is essential since it will help both of you to achieve your dreams. This also creates harmony between your couple relationship goals and your personal goals.

- You should ensure that your goals are attainable and specific.

- Always make sure that you have celebrated any achievements or milestone reached as a couple. This is a simple way to motivate both of you.

- You should stay accountable to all the commitments you made to each other. This should be so since this is a sacred bond between the partners and it is not a matter of punishment or reward. This is an arrangement that supports both of you as well as your relationship.

Reasons for setting common couple goals

1. They act as the glue that holds you together, even during the most challenging moments in your relationship.

2. It provides great satisfaction when goals are achieved, and it gives spouses reasons for them to celebrate together.

3. Goals validate desires and hold one accountable to each other.

4. Setting common goals improves communication since each person in the relationship is given a chance to talk about personal goals and dreams; by doing, so it helps the couple to understand each other better.

5. Helps the spouse or partner to strengthen their relationship by working together to achieve the common goals.

A few years ago, at the suggestion of a friend, Troy and I began the tradition of setting goals for our marriage at the beginning of each New Year. We have always set goals for our family, finances, fitness, business, and parenting, but as we began to grow as a couple, we recognized several areas for improvement and began to set ourselves marital goals.

It is common to set goals at work to increase productivity and, on a personal level, to improve health or achieve something of importance like financial security. We know the value of working towards goals because we've witnessed what can be accomplished when we're focused and driven. So why not set goals for our marriage, as well?

Setting goals together as a couple requires you to work as a team towards a common purpose which helps fortify your relationship. From day one, Troy has referred to us as a team. I love this concept because it is so easy to relate to and understand.

If a team wants to win, each player has to work together with the others, to do it. In marriage, your ultimate goal is to help one other become holy and get to heaven, but I think most couples would agree that being in a fulfilling, happy marriage is a WIN on this side of heaven!

So how do we WIN in marriage? Life happens; we get knocked down and sometimes forget that we are on the same team! Don't overlook the fact that you are on the same team if you want to win. Remembering this motivates me to get beyond a grudge I may be holding and move more swiftly towards reconciliation. Determine what you can do daily or even weekly to reinforce the fact that you are on the same team. Perhaps, similar to doing a daily examination of conscience, you can do a marital examination of conscience, either privately in your heart or together as a couple. Reflect on what you did well that day/week to love your spouse and what areas need improvement.

Come up with a marital game plan. Every team has a plan they try to follow that puts them in the best position to win. Good offense – what can you proactively do to help your marriage grow? Good defense – what hedges do you need to put around your marriage to protect it from damage?

Teammates are accountable to one another. If one teammate is in the wrong, it affects the entire team. It is the same in marriage: it is important to forgive but also to hold each other accountable. There is a difference between holding a grudge and holding your spouse accountable for a wrong that needs to be made right. Until this is done, your team cannot work in sync. If you desire a successful marital team, you need to admit when you are wrong. Your spouse shouldn't have to pull an apology out of you; it takes away the sincerity of it. Admit when you are wrong, so you don't have to play defense without purpose. If you are the spouse that is offended, forgive to get out of the offensive zone. Make it a goal to be accountable to one another for the sake of your marriage, your family, and your salvation.

In any team, when one player is down, another player steps up to the plate to fill in. A good goal you may choose to set for your marriage is to understand better how you can support your spouse when he or she is down. Are you loving and emotionally supportive? Do you help pick them up or do you ignore the fact that they are down, so you don't have to deal with it? Perhaps, because of your wounds, pride or lack of energy, you find it challenging to help your spouse when he or she is down in their game. This is when relying on the grace of the sacrament of marriage gives you the strength to live your vows "in good times and in bad."

I recently read a story about an experiment off the coast of Brazil. Two bottles were dropped in the ocean off a boat at the same time and right next to each other. One bottle washed up on the coast of Ecuador 100 days later and the other bottle went across the Atlantic Ocean and washed up on the coast of Tanzania a year later. The bottles started in the same place but ended up a half a world apart. It is the same in marriage – it is so easy to drift apart and not even realize you are doing it! Setting goals together and following through on their development will help you consciously stay close so that you do not end up half a world apart. If you want to prevent drift in your relationship, you must be intentional.

Can you set a goal to have a weekly date night or get away together for a few days? Troy and I try to go on a date at least 2-3 times a month, and we also get away somewhere alone once a year for a few days. This "date" time has been an enormous blessing for our marriage!

Set realistic goals and be flexible. Do what works for you and be mindful of the current season. Periodically take time to reevaluate your goals and redesign your plan if necessary. Life happens, and inevitably, something will cause you to get off track, but the critical thing to remember is to get back on track as soon as possible and make accommodations if a curveball is thrown your way. Celebrate your accomplishments.

Goal setting as a couple improves communication and assists couples in better understanding one other because it allows each spouse to express their dreams and desires for the marriage. There is less misunderstanding, resentment, and conflict since each person is heard and their needs validated. This, in turn, leads to a more fulfilling and happy marriage.

Chapter 10: Grow Together

You should make it your priority to evolve together, expecting each other in difficult times continually. Good communication is the key when it comes to growing together. Good communication involves spouses showing each other that they are listening. Having a conversation with someone who is utterly quiet can make one feel that they are conversing with themselves.

It is, therefore, important that every spouse contributes to show they are listening. For example, a spouse may add on to what the other person has said. This shows that everyone is listening attentively and processing the issues. If, for example, one person is talking about their day at work, the partner may say, "It sounds as if that office has some people with personal issuers rubbing off on everybody. The things that the secretary said would tick me off too". The person may also add "What can I do to make your day better." Language like this shows a partner that they have been understood and that they can get help if they need it.

Good communication is not all about talking and talking. Sometimes, the best medicine involves a good level of silence. For instance, when two people are having a conversation, they can take a break to digest what they have said to each other. The silence will help the two people put their thoughts in order and avoid blunting out things unintentionally. Open communication and conversation do not mean going on and on in an endless conversation. Take a break and a breath. Good silence also indicates to the partners that they are reflecting on all that has been said.

Good and open communication requires one to be

sensitive to the moods, schedules, and other factors of their partner. Select a good time to have an effective back and forth based on the conversation you want to have. However, things that need to be addressed should not be ousted too far off. Address matters openly as soon as possible because dwelling on them in silence will bring problems. One should pick a suitable moment as soon as possible and open up.

Another important factor that can help couples grow together is honoring the opinions of a partner even if they differ. Honoring different views is one of the main keys to good communication. To show honor of different opinions, one may say "I understand what you are saying, but I think... Can we agree to disagree?" Such statements will not only acknowledge that one person has understood the other but also that they respect a different opinion. They also help one state their different opinion without overstepping their boundaries. Honoring the views of each other de-escalates what could have become a conflict.

Couples need to identify ways of having the most productive conversations which will add value to their marriage. One of the best ways of maintaining an emotional connection is through holding good open conversations. Couples should segregate time to hold conversations and put some of the tips named above into practice. Six secrets that couples can use to grow together include:

✓ **They evaluate experiences**

"Experience is the greatest teacher" only if we assess them and consciously learn from our mistakes. Otherwise, we are likely to repeat them. In growth-oriented marriages, couples take that crucial step back and ask: What worked in this situation? What didn't work? What can we do better next time? They stop arguing. They stop paddling. They come up with a new plan.

✓ They learn to communicate in each other's language

We all grow up with different communication styles and inferences. Some of us are used to families where everyone directly expresses his feelings, and others are used to more round-about, sensitive ways of speaking. The key to growing in marriage is to learn to speak your spouse's language even if that isn't how you are used to communicating. We often have to learn and re-learn this habit, sometimes to listen when our instinct is to speak, to pause before we figure out how to say something and to think about what we're trying to accomplish with our words.

✓ They share what they learn

Whether it is an exciting story in the news, an idea from a Torah class they heard or something new that they learned at work, couples who grow together share what they learn each day. They make sure to discuss ideas and goals so that their connection doesn't become lost in errands, to do lists and family responsibilities.

✓ They see their relationship as multi-dimensional

There are many ways I identify who I am. Part of my identity is associated with my profession as a family therapist and as a writer. A substantial portion of who I am is an amalgam of being an athlete, a mother, a wife, and a religious Jew. All of these parts of me are essential to my identity and reinforce each other. A growing marriage has several dimensions to its identity too. There is the romantic dimension that first drew the couple together, the friendship that becomes stronger each year, the team identity we need for parenting, and the shared activities dimension in which growing couples hike or bike or attend a class together. Like the parts of our personalities, the aspects of a growing marriage strengthen and enhance each other.

✓ They know how to laugh together

Life can sometimes get very stressful. Your kids are fighting. Your teenager doesn't like school. An appliance breaks. There's an extra hour of traffic... the list can go on and on. We all have stress and challenges. One of the best tools growing couples use for stress is humor. They know how to laugh to break the tension. They know how to step back and see the big picture when things get hard. They have jokes that they share so that they can find the way forward, even when they're stuck in traffic.

✓ They plan adventures together

Growth-oriented couples love to try new things and go to different places. It doesn't take a lot of money to go camping together or to hike in a state park or watching the sunset over the ocean. But it takes enthusiasm and a desire to grow for couples to reach new realms in their lives and their marriages.

The importance of practicing day after day to achieve a mindful relationship

Communication in marriage and connection are directly related. Without one, the other is likely to fail. When people can express themselves adequately, things tend to be better even when they cannot agree on a particular subject. For instance, if a couple is talking about how much money they should spend on entertainment per month, the husband may want more to go to movies and games while the wife wants more to go with her girlfriends for shopping sprees. The couple may not initially agree on the amount they should spend, but so long as they are communicating about it, they both understand what the other wants. When communication is a challenge, one may feel that the other is being wasteful and still not express it in the right way. Bad communication leads to feelings of isolation, sadness, loneliness, heartbroken and disheartened.

Communication is important for both simple and tough reasons. In the movies, couples seem to have some almost perfect lives, but in the real world, it is more complicated than that. People have to make decisions about children, money, work life, obligations, and other action items without a screen script to follow. Such matters call on the couples to have deep conversations. Even the little things that could be ignored before the couple lives together have to be taken into consideration; otherwise, the marriage might fail. Without the right communication in marriage, drifts happen, and the couple that was ones so in love becomes strangers sharing a table. Again, communication in marriage differs from communication in a relationship because couples tend to get tired of the masks want to deal with real feelings. The spouses want to be heard; their deep needs start to surface; they want to be validated. If one person keeps dismissing, interrupting or shutting down their partner, there will be a rift between them.

Good communication leads to a great marriage and

more. As seen earlier, communication and connection go together and consequently if one goes down, the other fails too. Every couple should strive to revive the communication whenever there are hiccups because it will lead to stronger intimacy both physically and emotionally. Communication is not required in marriage just for emotional and physical connection. The couples also need to make decisions about development and growth.

In many cases, development and growth involve making decisions about money. When two people come together in marriage, there are a lot of emotions that get tied up in how they spend money. If therefore the couple keeps pushing aside conversations about money decisions, a lot of problems will arise soon in the family. Communication is also important because people only have a finite amount of time on earth- no one wants to be in a relationship where there is no connection. That is why many people opt for divorces when the spouses are no longer connected. One way to avoid separations and stay connected for a long time is to keep rediscovering things about one another more so through communication. Change for the better and show it to one another that you are putting effort to make it work. Share experiences, create new memories which you can discuss later and laugh. Good communication ensures that the couple knows which statements would make the other person shut down or build a wall; therefore, they avoid offending one another. Good communication is proactive such that, instead of waiting for things to go wrong to start a conversation, the couple sorts things out in time. The results of good communication are a solid foundation in the marriage where the couple can talk about anything without fear.

Many couples who have difficulties in communication think that it will take an arm and a leg to get back on track. Although this might be true for some broken communications, the majority of the couples need to make small steps towards better communication, and they will achieve a considerable difference. A few adjustments to the channels of communication and the spouses will achieve a tremendous compounding effect on their relationship and marriage. While facing communication challenges, many couples also tend to feel like they are the only ones undergoing this. It is important for them to remember that they are not the only ones facing challenges. Challenges are normal in every relationship. The key to solving the problems is consistency.

Remember, a distance between couples or any two people does not happen overnight. There is not just one reason which leads to a total drift in a couple that was once madly in love. It is a result of small omissions and commissions that offend the other person, therefore, creating mountains of differences and gaps between the two people. In the initial stages of a relationship and marriage, a couple can easily thrive on excitement and physical attraction, therefore, communication plays a small role and many of its aspects will be ignored.

As the bond between the two individuals deepens, the attraction changes very fast into the first stages of love where every person is making a foundation of trust. This is because they want to have a stronger and happier future. When in marriage, the love that once thrived on attraction and excitement changes to one that is sustained by trust, commitment, and honesty. Over the years, the responsibilities change, and the amount of stress increases with an increase in challenges. Somehow, the time to be there for one another and to share seems to diminish.

Communication becomes a chore that couples would rather skip even if it is talking about a joyous moment. Things seem to change, and the couples that thought marriage is a completely smooth ride usually feel cheated or lost. The suppressed negative feelings that arise from this situation make a couple preys to miscommunication or total lack of it. Then the drift occurs, followed by assumption and mistrusts, in worse cases infidelity, lack of respect, dishonesty, et cetera. Good communication means that a couple respects one another enough to stay honest.

Demystifying the fairytales

In all healthy relationships, communication must act as the centerpiece. All individuals in all relationships whether in marriage or workplace must maintain good communication and check in regularly. Marriages consist of more than just keeping a household, parenting and taking care of bills. With time, the couple begins to understand that the fairy tale- happily ever after has many holes and it takes a lot of effort from both sides to make it work.

In real life, knights on horses rarely ride in and rescue damsels in distress to a happily ever after situation. Consequently, it is important for spouses to remember to talk to one another rather than at each other. Married Couples are in a full-time job called marriage where they should always love and appreciate each other to achieve their marriage goals. The difficult part is that most of the spouses in marriages do not know how to alter their mentality to accommodate real life things that make marriages work. That is why when many couples have difficulties communicating; they focus on the divorce statistics and the number of maintenance cases in the courts. When the spouses realize that the number of cases is too high, they get into panic mode and set the same expectations for their own homes. This expectations and standards tend to kill the marriages that would otherwise thrive.

It is wrong for people to use what is happening around them to gauge their marriages. Most of the statists given to the public only involve detrimental unions. They hardly tell people of the winning marriages and how they got there. In other words, those offering statistics to the public do not tell them what it takes for the marriages to fail or succeed. They fail to discuss the satisfaction levels and communication in marriages, and therefore people do not realize that most marriages fail because of things that would be solved through communication.

Every couple has one thing that they try to avoid conversing about therefore they dance around the matter to avoid conflict. It could be love, sex, or money, but in every relationship, there is that one thing that causes disagreements, and because of the conflicting nature, couples opt not to put the matter to rest. For example, one spouse could want to save money while the other one wants to spend, one wants more sex, while the other one is happy about the current situation et cetera. This results in more conflict.

Arguing in marriages

Communication plays a vital role in any relationship, and it is one of the main pillars of marriage. Arguments and disagreements are also a part of healthy relationships but the success of failure if the differences lie in how the two parties engage each other to settle things.

Couples should understand that arguing is not always unhealthy. It is better than staying silent because lack of communication leads to assumptions, confusion, dissatisfaction, and more misunderstandings. When arguments are done constructively, they help the couple grow. Every spouse should strive to find out more about what their partner wants and thinks. There are many ways of disagreeing healthily and be sure that two people cannot always be in synch. IF a couple is always on the same page in all matters, then one person is faking or ignoring their personal feelings for the sake of the other. In the long term, this setting aside of feelings for the sake of the other person will lead to intense conflicts. Every spouse should look out for the signs that the other person is ignoring their feelings and help them reason together without hiding matters.

When a couple sets aside the blame games and assesses their issues and troubles from a wider perspective, they will easily identify where their different desires overlap. Once the individuals have identified where the opinions overlap, they can come up with agreements. Identifying the point where two people overlap helps them solve the matters faster that when each of them was set on individually. The couple should be affirmative and specific with their agreements to ensure that both parties are on board and that they understand their next step.

Conclusion

Thank you for making it to the end of the book *Communication for Couples*: Discover how to *hear Your Partner to Achieve a Healthy Relationship, Improve Mindful Habits, and Grow Empathy for Each Other.* Let us hope that it was informative and that it provided you with all the tools you need to meet your goals irrespective of what they may be. Just because you have finished reading the book does not mean that there is nothing else to learn about the topic. Expanding your horizons is the only way that you can master what you have learned.

The next step is to stop reading and get started with doing what is required of you to ensure that those who depend on you are well taken care of. Put what you have learned into consideration and teach your friends the techniques you have acquired herein. If you find that you need to clarify some things in the book, feel free to read again and do some more research on the topic. Take responsibility for your actions and follow some of the tips you have gathered to improve your relationship with your partner.

Remember, communication keeps connections alive. Make it a habit to compliment your partner; keep the intimacy alive, keep the communication open, look for soft emotions, and rekindle that spark. It's about the two of you; therefore, do not seek to control every outcome in conversations and other sectors of life. Assuming that you do not want to get a divorce, do not threaten your spouse with one. In marriages, people get tempted to make threats of divorce during arguments. Do not! Use the tips in this book to pass your message efficiently.

Do not forget to download other series of books: *Communication Skills for Couples*, *Effective Communication, and Communication Skills Training*. All books form one bundle. I am sure you will enjoy the other series of books too.

Finally, if you found this book useful in any way, we would appreciate a review on Amazon!

SOURCES OF INFORMATION

https://healthypsych.
com/18-communication-tips-for-couples/

https://www.loveisrespect.org/healthy-relationships/
communicate-better/

https://www.psychalive.org/
top-10-effective-communication-techniques-couples/

https://psychcentral.com/
lib/5-communication-pitfalls-and-pointers-for-couples/

www.ingramcontent.com/pod-product-compliance
Lightning Source LLC
Chambersburg PA
CBHW071114030426
42336CB00013BA/2084